DISCARDED

D1525343

LAW LIFE AND LETTERS

VOLUME ONE

LAW LIFE AND LETTERS

DA
566.9
B 5
A 25
1970
vol. 1

999179

BY THE RIGHT HONOURABLE THE

EARL OF BIRKENHEAD

(FREDERICK EDWIN SMITH)

IN TWO VOLUMES

VOLUME ONE

LTL ᒪAMAR TECH ᒪIBRARY

Essay Index Reprint Series

BOOKS FOR LIBRARIES PRESS
FREEPORT, NEW YORK

First Published 1927
Reprinted 1970

STANDARD BOOK NUMBER:
8369-1450-3

LIBRARY OF CONGRESS CATALOG CARD NUMBER:
71-104997

PRINTED IN THE UNITED STATES OF AMERICA

TO
MY DAUGHTER
ELEANOR

CONTENTS

I

THE GLADSTONE CASE AND COGNATE TOPICS

IT is not my purpose to revive a discussion of the personal issues which made the recent libel action brought by Captain Peter Wright against Lord Gladstone so notoriòus. The case is over. The penalty for failure has been paid. The memory of a great man has been vindicated, to the satisfaction, it may be said without exaggeration, of the whole civilised world.

But the case has raised a number of topics of general interest which deserve a somewhat more careful examination than was possible during its hearing.

Incidentally, the litigation was of a very topsy-turvy kind. The general rule, which I will presently examine a little more closely, that when the dead are libelled no action can be brought, made it necessary that Lord Gladstone should publish statements *prima facie* defamatory of Captain Wright, in order that it might be determined whether or not the late Mr. Gladstone had led an immoral life. Had the rule of law been different, the legal process would naturally have been simpler. Lord Gladstone would either have brought a civil action claiming damages from Captain Wright, or he would have instituted criminal proceedings demanding fine or imprisonment.

In a civil proceeding for damages it is necessary, for a defendant who says that the defamatory statement is true, to prove that the statement complained of is true ; for, as a learned Judge once tersely observed, no man is entitled to damages for injury to a character which he has no right to possess.

But in criminal proceedings for libel the matter stands differently. Here, in the conception of the law, defamation is punishable because of its tendency to provoke a breach of the peace. Accordingly it is familiar law that a man may be found guilty of an indictment for criminal libel even though that which he wrote was true. And indeed, once you admit that the gravamen of the charge is the tendency of the libel complained of to provoke a breach of the peace, it must be conceded that it is at least as likely to produce such a breach if in fact it is true. But here, again, an exception has been admitted. The publication of a statement *prima facie* defamatory may be justified if two things are established : first, that it is true ; and secondly, that its publication is in the public interest.

It was for a long time supposed, though never very authoritatively decided, that an indictment would lie for a libel against the dead if its publication was of a kind likely, in the ordinary experience of reasonable men, to provoke the family of the dead man to a breach of the peace.

And indeed, the *Law Journal*, in an interesting article, has recently suggested that the right of action should be recognised by law where there is a libel upon the dead. The proposals would evidently require restrictions and safeguards, but these need not detain us here.

I will presently examine the merits of such a suggestion ; but before doing so I will shortly re-state the history of the matter.

The leading cases on the subject are R. *v.* Topham, which was tried so long ago as 1791, and R. *v.* Labouchere, which was tried in 1882. The matter was, however, more recently examined by Mr. Justice Stephen in R. *v.* Ensor, a case determined on circuit in the year 1887. The case was of a newspaper libel on a political opponent who had been dead for three years. The issues, therefore, were less obvious than in the Labouchere case, in which the Duke of Vallombrosa complained of a libel upon his grandfather, a contemporary of Napoleon. The Ensor libel in fact led to an assault by the dead man's sons upon the supposed libeller. The learned Judge has himself described the matter in the following language :

" I directed an acquittal, on the ground that no evidence was offered to show that the libel in any way referred to any living person."

I do not think that it can be argued that this was a satisfactory direction. It would in effect mean that there could not in any circumstances be a punishable libel on the dead. And indeed, the learned Judge himself, who was extraordinarily competent in such matters, has added the following observation :

" I ought to have added, but I did not do so clearly, that there was no evidence that the defendant wished to provoke the sons of the deceased. It was not even stated that he knew of their existence. I thought that an act with intent to injure (I should have added) or to provoke or annoy the sons was essential to the effects, and that a mere tendency to provoke or constructive intention inferred from the fact that the libel was calculated to hurt the feelings of any surviving relations of the deceased was not enough. . . . "

And accordingly the learned Judge, in his scholarly and scientific *Digest of the Criminal Law*, stated the rule, as he believed it to be, in the following words :

" The publication of a libel on the character of a dead person is not a misdemeanour unless it is intended to injure or provoke living persons."

I should much like to have the question argued before me, sitting in the House of Lords, whether the direction could be supported.

In the first place, ought the intention of the libeller to be made the decisive question ? Must not a man, here again, be presumed to intend the natural consequences of his acts ? Is not the true test whether the language used was or was not, in the opinion of reasonable people (as represented by the jury), likely to produce a breach of the peace ?

If such be a sound view of the law, the proposal made by the *Law Journal* is hardly needed. I do not attempt a decided statement as to whether or not Mr. Justice Stephen was right or wrong. He was a very acute and a very learned Judge ; and it is unsafe to express opinions *in abstracto* upon legal matters which have not been argued before one.   But I think the matter very arguable ; and the dicta in Rex *v*. Hunt (a much earlier case) were contradictory.

However this may be, it would certainly not be consistent with the conception of the offence of criminal libel that a prosecution for libel on the dead should be recognised further than the view of the law, which I have indicated as possible, would warrant.

But if the law were laid down in the following way :

" The publication of a libel on the character of a dead person is not a misdemeanour unless it is calculated to injure or provoke living persons,"

nearly every reasonable mischief would be cured. It is, for instance, obvious that no one would think it necessary to enable the descendants (if there be any) of " Judge " Jeffreys to bring an action against a modern biographer who had formed an unfavourable view of the moral character of this energetic Judge.

I observe from the Press that a less extreme but still a remarkable attempt of the same kind is being made in France by the granddaughter of George Sand, who is bringing proceedings against a modern author who has alleged moral frailty against her distinguished grandmother.

I offer, naturally, no opinion upon the law of France. But I should have thought that in any country there must be a reasonable law of limitations in such matters. The resentment of a son, for instance, may be as warm and as reasonable as it most plainly was in the case of Lord Gladstone. That of a grandson would naturally be more remote ; and it is difficult to conceive that a great-grandson would in any circumstances be entitled to repel by violence criticisms which he happened to dislike directed at his great-grandfather.

The formula which I have suggested would meet all these difficulties. The question for the jury would be : were the words complained of " calculated to injure or provoke living persons " ? And the jury would naturally be told in the direction that they were to consider themselves as dealing with normal, sensible, living persons and not with descendants abnormal, hyper-sensitive, or more vindictive than the common run.

If the law had been declared in the sense of these observations, Lord Gladstone would have brought his action. The Judge would have asked the jury the question above proposed. I

cannot doubt that the jury would have answered
it affirmatively, and so the matter would have
ended with a direct and logical conclusion founded
upon true and not upon artificial issues.

So much for the legal considerations involved.
Wider social and literary implications deserve
attention. There is here both a Scylla and a
Charybdis; the Scylla of *de mortuis nil nisi
bonum*, and the Charybdis of fidelity to history.
It is entirely creditable to the fundamental
decency of most people that they should have an
instinct not to defame, or, as Dr. Johnson might
have said, to denigrate, the characters of persons
who are no longer able to defend themselves.
Mortalia pectora tangunt: and those are happily
few in number who wish to push animosity or
disparagement into the grave of a corpse.

But here, again, the doctrine can only be laid
down with limitations. To take an extreme case,
Judas Iscariot could hardly have escaped the
criticism of the ages by founding himself upon this
maxim. There comes a time when history claims
its own. And here it must be conceded that a
difference is to be reasonably drawn between
those who have played a great part in the public
eye, with all its anxieties and all its compensations,
and those who have been content with private

careers. A man who undertakes public life is rather like a man who publishes a book. Within reasonable limits he challenges observation and relevant criticism. And indeed he very frequently makes it about others. He has become a brick, considerable or inconsiderable, in the majestic building of political or literary history. Such a one cannot claim that the candid and honest examination of his career should cease with his death. He has deliberately played for a great and a public stake. Just, therefore, as his acts and general character reasonably challenged, and received, attention in his lifetime, so in due relation to the interest and importance of his career must he expect that an unmalicious dissection will continue after his death.

But I am bound with deep respect to make it plain that, in my opinion, Mr. Justice Horridge, a very careful Judge, pushed these considerations much too far in the Bath Club case. The learned Judge told the jury that " Mr. Gladstone, having sought and obtained a great public position, is not entitled to object to criticism." This direction surely involves a most unfortunate confusion of thought, and indeed a misuse of language. When did Mr. Gladstone object to criticism of himself ? When did Lord Gladstone object to

criticism of his father ? Criticism, in the sense
in which we are concerned with the term, means the
passing of judgment on qualities ; upon merits and
demerits. It does not mean, and it never has
meant, the making of unprovable and highly
defamatory statements of fact in relation to a
dead man of distinction.

We must however—speaking now not as lawyers
but merely as persons interested in certain social,
public, and literary problems—attempt to adjust
these two conflicting points of view.

An ingenious writer in *Truth*, in a recent article
upon this subject, has made the following observation :

" To impose upon all writers and speakers the
adamantine rule that they shall make no allusion
to departed greatness which is not couched in
terms of flattery or approbation, is to set a mischievous premium on hypocrisy and falsehood.
Nor is it easy to draw a clear line of demarcation
between private character and public conduct.
The morals of a statesman, for example, are no
mere trivial accident, but an integral part of his
personality, as it presents itself to the eye of the
historian. A rule which is to serve as a universal
guide for posthumous commentators must be
broad, comprehensive, troubled with no subtle
distinctions, easy to grasp and apply. Can such
a rule be found ? I think it can. At any rate,

I would venture to suggest as a good enough working proposition for an imperfect world that whenever an historian, memoir writer, journalist, or any self-appointed censor of defunct humanity ventures to canvass the honour and reputation of deceased persons, he should be at pains patiently to inform himself of the facts, *using every available avenue of information*, and when research has furnished him *with undeniable knowledge*, though not till then, he should be at liberty to tell the truth."

These observations seem to me to be very sensible ; but they are perhaps too general to afford us all the guidance that we require. Who, for instance, in dealing with the past, could define " undeniable knowledge " ? Who has it of the Casket letters ? How much knowledge is " undeniable " ? How, in such a context, are we to define the words " every available avenue of information " ? Every " available avenue " may be inadequate.

Perhaps we might go a little further, while accepting the general reasonableness of the passage which I have quoted. Two circumstances in this consideration are of first-class, perhaps even of decisive, importance.

The first question which I should ask myself in such a matter would be this : Was the knowledge or the suspicion upon which the criticism of the dead man was founded available for his critics while he still lived and could have defended his own honour ?

If it clearly was, and nobody ever dared in any public manner to make the charge while he lived, does not that supply us with an almost irresistible bias against him who brings the charges after death ?

Let me develop this view a little. No one has ever disputed Mr. Gladstone's enormous courage. I cannot discover at any period of his life—though I have no particular sympathy with his career— that he ever allowed fear or nervousness to deflect him from any course on which he was otherwise determined. His controversial powers and combative resources have hardly been exceeded. Is it not altogether intolerable that on suspicions well-known, subterraneously bruited, and generally contemned, in his own lifetime, he should be defamed when his own voice is stilled in death, and when nearly all those who equally had knowledge of the facts are no longer, for the same melancholy reason, available witnesses ?

I said that a second point arose, which may perhaps be treated as an exceptional case overriding the considerations referred to above.

If entirely new evidence emerges through what one must conceive of as some historical accident, which seems decisive in its character, and which was not available to the dead man's contemporaries, there may be, for those who like it, a real excuse for assuming the rôle of historical disparager. But it must surely in any event be wrong to publish charges against a dead man when no information of any kind is available which did not exist in his lifetime ; and when the evidence must, from the very nature of the case, have dwindled continuously since his death.

An observation may be added of a more general character. It is really, if one analyses it, an altogether terrible thing to bring pain and suffering into the surviving family of one whom they have loved and revered. His greatness and his reputation have probably been the greatness, pride, and happiness of their own lives. To assault him after death is surely to defile the very fountains of kindliness, of piety, and of decency.

Other matters have recently engaged the public attention, which, though less dramatic, are not wholly unrelated to the issues of the Gladstone case. I found myself, for instance, recently involved in controversy with two friends, Lady Oxford and Mr. Arnold Bennett, on a subject of

some importance, affecting on the one hand
writers of memoirs like Lady Oxford, on the other
novelists like Mr. Arnold Bennett. I do not
revive the dispute with Mr. Bennett as to whether
or not Lord Raingo can properly be identified
with a statesman recently deceased. It is sufficient for me that his journalistic sponsors told us
so, and Mr. Arnold Bennett, at a critical moment,
did not dispute a very profitable claim.

The two cases are distinguishable.

Let me, then, deal first with the practice to which
Lady Oxford has, with admitted good faith, had
extensive recourse, that of quoting long conversations—for instance, with General Booth, Dr.
Jowett, Lord Salisbury, and Mr. Gladstone, none
of whom, of course, is now alive. It is to be
noticed that the gifted authoress of these memoirs
seldom comes off second best in the discussion.
In a homely phrase, she " holds up her end "
surprisingly well when confronted by such versatile and even *rusé* conversationalists. The
dialogues in almost every case purport to be given
verbatim.

But how many of us can remember with any
exact reliability a long conversation which we
had even a month ago ? How few of us are really
able to resist the temptation, when quoting from

any controversial talk in which we have become involved, of giving ourselves, in the account of the matter, just a little the best of the exchange ?

And it is, of course, perfectly obvious that none of the distinguished men concerned can ever have been told that it was this vivacious and undefeated lady's purpose, years after they were dead, to produce these conversations with an appearance of verbal precision. Nearly all great men are quite vain. And if any one of these four had known how considerable was to be the future vogue and influence of Lady Oxford, and that she intended one day to publish detailed accounts of conversations between themselves and her, I very strongly suspect that they would have suggested the reasonableness of a written exchange of recollections in the matter.

I may, of course, be asked how I reconcile these views with the practice of the greatest biographer of all, James Boswell. Pepys's Diary belongs to a different class, for I am sure that, on the whole, much as there is to be said for the other view, he did not desire or contemplate its publication.

But of Boswell it will undoubtedly be said that almost the whole of his book is taken up with extracts from his hero's conversations. And it cannot be denied that the hero was dead. But surely there was a very plain distinction. It was well known to the Doctor that Boswell was his idolatrous, almost his undiscriminating admirer. And I suspect also that Johnson knew that, quite apart from the other's genuine friendship and devotion, his proposed biographer discerned for himself in the prospect of an immortal work the only real hope he could have had of an undying literary distinction.

He had of course a sturdy and manly pride in the value of his talk. Nor with Boswell was he running much risk.

At any rate, Johnson, who often saw more than he appeared to see, was for years in the company of Boswell while Boswell was taking faithful and even ostentatious notes of his opinions and of the language in which he expressed them. He was well aware that Boswell intended to write about him. On one occasion the Scotsman asked him to give him some chronological account of his early life for the purposes of this very book, to which the great man replied that the author would no doubt collect it by degrees from his conversation. If a man, when alive, makes choice of a particular friend, gives him every assistance, allows his conversation to be taken down, and speaks with complacency of his friend's biographical intention, he must surely be taken to have given permission for that other to recount his talk, and to be willing to take the risk that he may not always be reproduced with precise accuracy.

It is evident, however, that Lady Oxford never contemplated producing the life-story of either General Booth, Dr. Jowett, Lord Salisbury, or Mr. Gladstone. And it is, I suppose, equally evident that none of these gentlemen ever asked her to undertake this task. Each of them, I think, would have contemplated the prospect with anxiety.

I incline, therefore, to the view that the wiser course is, never to publish conversations with dead people, for human nature is very fallible. They are no longer here to give their own version. Still less should one do so when, on the whole, the narration rather redounds to one's own credit. If you repeat such talk at all, let it be in circumstances which are entirely favourable to those who can no longer give their own account. I have, for instance, myself in my own writings on two or three occasions repeated very genuine conversations which I had both with the late Lord Kitchener and with the late Mr. Joseph Chamberlain. But on neither occasion did I myself come particularly well out of the discussion. And I am certain that the descendants and relatives of the distinguished men with whom I was dealing felt no grievance, but rather gratitude for that which I had written.

Another illustration may be given before passing altogether from this topic. A distinguished, correct, and very careful lawyer, Professor Morgan, in a most interesting sketch which he published of the late Lord Morley, quoted a particular conversation which bears upon the present subject. Lord Morley, the Professor recalls, told him that Lord Granville had once made the statement that five of Queen Victoria's Prime Ministers had been guilty of adultery. Professor Morgan has since, in a letter to the *Times*, so candidly recognised the danger of this kind of writing, that he will not be offended by a slight analysis, first, of the theoretic objections to the repetition of a statement of this kind, and then of its practical reactions.

In the first place, the matter depends upon hearsay at fourth- or fifth-hand.

It is hearsay in relation to what a dead man is reported to have said.

On what authoritative evidence does the statement that Lord Granville ever said anything of the kind depend ? Who heard him say it ? In what contemporary document is it recorded ?

It becomes, in the next place, necessary to ask, who told Lord Morley that Lord Granville had said it ? Did Lord Morley's informer claim that he had it himself from Lord Granville ? If not, it must at once be plainly realised that there were probably five or six hearsay links in the chain even before it reached Lord Morley.

A further observation may usefully be made. If Lord Granville ever did make the charge (as to which I am absolutely sceptical), was he a man who, in a spirit of pleasantry and for the sake of producing a sensation in society, was in the habit of saying daring and paradoxical things ?

The theoretical objections, then, stare one in the face to the publicaton of charges or reflections alleged to have been made by one dead man upon another.

The practical inconveniences are obviously quite intolerable. If the charge appears to be vouched upon high authority, the descendants and the biographers of all Queen Victoria's Prime Ministers may reasonably be expected to busy themselves about the matter. And no one will ever reach an absolutely authoritative conclusion. That such inquiries should ever be rendered necessary, with the anxiety and unpleasantness involved, where the whole charge really depends upon eighth-rate conversational hearsay, is of course both ludicrous and intolerable.

And observe an illustration of the possible results. The plaintiff in the Gladstone case fastens upon the charge supposed to have been made by Lord Granville; reinforces it by the authority which he attempts to borrow from Lord Morley; and finally attempts more or less to affiliate it upon the cool judgment and respectable literary methods of a contemporary lawyer.

Quite a new and closely allied matter is presented by the practice which has recently become fashionable of writing novels which deal in one way or another with persons either still living or recently dead.

Such a habit was very well known to the lampoonists and comedians of ancient Athens. Aristophanes, for instance, in his brilliant plays, was in the habit of producing both Socrates and his great tragic contemporaries upon the comic stage.

But on the whole the practice has not been adopted by our greater novelists. The art of writing great romances is in the main imaginative. It differs from the art of the historian, the memoir writer, or the journalist. The very necessity of drawing upon living men to lend a point to your story indicates a certain bankruptcy in the more essential equipment of a great romantic writer.

But as I am anxious to avoid unnecessary controversy I will attempt upon this point, too, a generalisation. It is altogether wrong for a novelist under a thin disguise to bring into his stories in any circumstances of disparagement one who is alive or recently dead, in a matter which was never proved against him in his lifetime, and which must bring much unhappiness to his descendants. I did not myself, though an ardent admirer of Mr. Arnold Bennett's more normal stories, succeed in reading *Lord Raingo* throughout. But I read enough to show me very clearly who Lord Raingo was intended to be.

Had the original of this character been alive, able to satisfy the jury that the characterisation attempted was intended to reflect upon him and was defamatory, he could have sheltered himself under the authority of the House of Lords in the Artemus Jones case,[1] and brought an action to recover damages for libel.

I observe, while I am upon this point, that Lord Gorell has just introduced into the House of Lords a Bill with the object of correcting the famous decision in that case.

[1] Hulton *v.* Jones, 1910, A.C. 20.

I have always been interested in the doctrines laid down, for I was offered the leading brief for the *Sunday Chronicle* at the Manchester Assizes. And accordingly I followed the later stages of the litigation with great care.

I came to the conclusion that the decision of the House of Lords was defensible in relation to the facts of the particular case, but that the dicta of more than one of their lordships were far too widely laid down. There were in the history of the case special reasons why a particular paper dealing with a name so unusual as Artemus Jones, —and so well known in the district where the paper circulated—should have avoided its employment in a discreditable or at least a light atmosphere. And accordingly no harm would have been done if the decision had merely laid it down that on the facts of this particular case the defendants had libelled the plaintiff because they either knew, or ought to have known, that the statements complained of would be associated with him by many of those who were fellow-townsmen of both.

But I never agreed with the general doctrine laid down ; and indeed, the brilliant dissenting judgment of Lord Fletcher Moulton corresponded almost exactly with the view which I formed then, and to which I still adhere.

Mr. Wells's Clissold book falls under a different heading. I never like uttering a word of criticism, however light, of a writer who has given me so much pleasure as this various and gifted author. The prescience and the inventiveness of his scientific stories have nothing to fear from a comparison with those of Jules Verne. The delineation of character in his romances proper is as subtle as his resource is infinite and his literary style brilliant.

But I must confess that where I admire him most is for the extraordinary skill with which he has succeeded in foisting off tiresome pamphlets upon the reviewers and the public in the guise of romances. That he should have done so with success is indeed an extraordinary tribute to the kind of chloroforming position to which he has attained.

The World of William Clissold is a good illustration of this very unusual facility. Mr. Clissold is, of course, Mr. Wells. That would not be too bad, though a little fatiguing, if there were not two Mr. Clissolds ; and if they were not both Mr. Wells. Those who know this writer can conceive the sheer delight with which, having duplicated the instruments whereby he expresses his own dogmas, his own cocksureness, and his own superiority, he becomes the publicity agent of his own turns. Messrs. Wells Brothers, in fact, examine many considerable personages in our national life ; they are measured in the Clissold scale ; are found lacking according to the Wells standard ; and are flung aside in contempt.

The matter under discussion here is quite distinct from those heretofore considered. I happen myself to object to the method, not because of the personalities involved—I take no objection, for instance, to anything that Mr. Wells says about me—but because artistically, and from the point of view of romantic writing as hitherto understood, the method adopted seems to me tiresome, dull, sterile, and irritating.

The methods of advertising also, a very questionable side of art adopted by Mr. Wells and by his publishers with his consent, seem to me to be both blatant and indelicate.

Mr. Wells is very lavish in his criticism of other people. He is contemptuous of the more vulgar artifices of self-advertisement. Yet two very important papers, the *Observer* and the *Daily Express*, were favoured with an advance notice of Mr. Wells's new novel. " Famous Statesmen Criticised " was one of the headlines. Mr. Victor Gollancz, managing director of Ernest Benn, Ltd., was obliging enough to give us a forecast of the book.

His disinterested recommendation, expressed in almost identical language in both newspapers, is interesting. " I believe," says this independent critic, " that this novel will create discussion and controversy even greater than that created by *William Clissold* last autumn." Well, this might easily be ; for the only controversy which had its origin in William Clissold was how so tiresome a book (even when trumpeted by silver-tongued Mr. Gollancz) succeeded in fooling so many competent reviewers. But hear Mr. Gollancz further and not even, be it observed, in an advertisement column : " The very centre of this novel is an absolutely ruthless criticism of the Conservative Government and particularly of Mr. Baldwin and Mr. Churchill for their conduct of the coal dispute."

Imagine Thackeray or George Eliot or any real artist :

(1) impelled by poverty of imaginative re-source to recommend a novel by the pres-tige and reputation, *ex hypothesi* greater than his own, of famous public men ;

(2) finding it necessary to persuade the publisher to purvey these nauseating

preliminary puffs of a book which, if it sells at all, will sell only because the public is interested not in the author, but in the personalities out of which he makes his living.

Incidentally also Mr. Wells might inform us " in his own brilliant style" (Mr. Gollancz), what he himself did, and where he stood, in the General Strike. I suspect exactly what Mr. Britling did in the Great War. He did not see it through either way. He continually escapes, or is incapable of, executive responsibility, and then makes money (in large terms for a Socialist) out of those who have discharged it and incurred the risks of failure.

A last and very difficult subject upon which I make a few observations is concerned with the recent growth of semi-scandalous volumes of memoirs. The late Lady Cardigan's notorious volume, though not the first of the class, has proved the forerunner of many others. Here the most scandalous insinuations are made about dead people, either mentioned by name or else thinly disguised.

The *Memoirs of Harriette Wilson* supply a memorial of a woman, one must suppose, infinitely more charming than Lady Cardigan. This remarkable woman was the daughter of John Dubochet. Some great quality must have existed in the family, for four most beautiful women were born as sisters. Harriette was unique. She was lovely and charming ; she was extremely intelligent without being intellectual. She had many of the mental and physical qualities of Lady Hamilton. And like Lady Hamilton she substituted for a precision school of ethics a gay (and a very ancient) philosophy.

She was the loyal and faithful friend of many men of the utmost distinction alike in rank and public service. But, like Mr. Bennett and Mr. Wells and Lady Cardigan, she one day found it profitable to exploit the reputation of persons more important than herself. Indeed, her interesting, even if scandalous, memoirs far excel the almost contemporary effort of " A Young Lady of Quality."

That our delightful friend was capable of sinking to blackmail I cannot doubt. But she would not, I think, have done so unless confronted by very grave necessity. She was on analysis very light yet very fascinating. Like Becky Sharp, she could have been a very good girl on £5,000 a year (pre-War).

I must add the evidence of her weakness, even

1—3

in a sentence in which I do justice to her strength. Her relations with His Grace the Duke of Wellington are, I think, plainly established. That in the end she intended to make money out of them is, I think, at least equally plain. Take the following passage :

" Unfortunately, Stockdale, in a courteous fit, acquainted the immortal Wellington that I was about to publish part of his private life, under the impression, of course, that every act which relates to so great a hero must be interesting.

" Will it ever be believed ? His Grace, in the meek humility of his heart, has written to menace a prosecution if such trash be published. What trash, my dear Wellington ? Now, I will admit, for an instant, and it is really very good of me, that you are an excellent judge of literature, and could decide on the merits or demerits of a work with better taste and judgment than the first of Edinburgh reviewers. Still, in order to pronounce it trash, we should fancy that even Wellington himself must throw a hasty glance on one of its pages at least. Quite the contrary. Wellington knows himself to be the subject, and therefore wisely prejudges the book trash one fortnight before it sees the light ! So far so good ! But when my own Wellington, who has sighed over me, and groaned over me by the hour, talked of my wonderful beauty, ran after me, bribed Mrs. Porter over and over again, after I refused to listen to her overtures, only for a single smile from his beautiful Harriette ! Did he not kneel ? And was I not the object of his first, his most ardent wishes, on his arrival from Spain ? Only it was such a pity that Argyle got to my house first. No matter ! Though Argyle was not his rose, he had dwelled with it ; therefore, what could my tender swain Wellington do better than stand in the gutter at two in the morning pouring forth his amorous wishes in the pouring rain, in strains replete with the most heart-rending grief, to the favoured and fortunate lover who had supplanted him, as Stockdale has indulged me by getting so inimitably delineated. When, I say, this faithful lover, whose love survived six winters, six frosts, six chilling, nay, killing frosts, when Wellington sends the ungentle hint to my publisher, of hanging me, beautiful, adored and adorable me, on whom he had so often hung ! *Alors je pends la tête !* Is it thus he would immortalise me ? "

Nor, as the recent exposure of *The Whispering Gallery* by the *Daily Mail* reminds us, do the living escape in the more unscrupulous of these compilations. It is not infrequently discoverable that the writers of these memoirs are quite incapable of authorship, and possess no knowledge of the English language. Sometimes the books are notoriously not written by those social personages who lend their names, but by some literary hack happily gifted by Nature for this low purpose.

This habit of retailing or inventing garbage has grown a great deal in recent years. It certainly requires drastic correction. The blame is to be distributed in almost equal proportions between the publishers and a certain section of the reading public. That section of the public is blameworthy because it supplies a constant market for this kind of objectionable publication. A certain number of publishers are blameworthy because they have been willing to sail rather near the wind in the attempt to give that particular public the kind of literature it wants.

The courageous exposure on the part of the *Daily Mail* of the genesis of *The Whispering Gallery* did indeed very rapidly drive that indescribable book from circulation in this country. But it must be remembered that it continued to circulate freely for many months in the United States of America, giving an impression to American readers of life in this country as unattractive as it was untrue.

II

STRAY THOUGHTS ON LETTER-WRITING

I

" I AM too busy to-day to write you a short letter," so Mme de Staël excused herself to her daughter, on an occasion when pressure of work prevented her from packing into her concise, telling phrases the facts and thoughts, the words of encouragement and warning, which she was wont to convey. To-day it would seem that letter-writing, short or long, good or bad, is a declining, if not a decayed, art. I pass over the particular type of person—generally, and therefore the more unfortunately, a young person—who avowedly never answers a letter, be the missive an invitation to dinner, a parental injunction, or a tradesman's solicitude.

The staggering burden of the postman grows daily larger, and the number of notes, circulars, newspapers, and postal cards can be counted by thousands of millions ; but how often does he deliver what our forbears would dignify as a

Letter?   The telephone and the motor-car have so speeded up and short-circuited communication, that the method of transmitting thoughts and opinions—or even official instructions—by means of pen, ink, and paper has actually become both tedious and ineffective.   It is probable that Lord Aberdeen personally used more stationery while he held the reins of office for eleven months in the Crimean War than Lord Oxford and Mr. Lloyd George did between them during the great world-struggle ; and one shudders to think of the acres of very rough paper over which the Duke of Wellington drove that tireless quill.   The Duke would write a memorandum of twenty pages, and copy it out in his own hand amid a hundred imperious preoccupations.   Imagination recoils at the idea of Mr. Winston Churchill (for instance) embracing such purely manual labour.   The manuscripts of Charles Dickens and Walter Scott suggest that these authors must have been immune from— or else perpetual martyrs to—writer's cramp. Henry James is popularly supposed to have been the first to avoid any such risk by dictating direct to a stenographer—a fact which, as much as any peculiar subtlety of mind, may explain the length and complexity of his sentences. Mr. Edgar Wallace, too, it is understood, dictates his almost continuous (and very different) output to a typist, who must by now be *blasé* from perpetual thrills. Mr. H. G. Wells and Mr. John Buchan (I attempt no valuation, but reverently take note of the methods of those who *succeed*) write all with their own hands.

The only *public* man within my knowledge who discards the typewriter, disdains the dictaphone, and whenever possible dispenses with an amanuensis, is the present French Prime Minister. Magazine articles, books, copious—though always coherent and often pungent—letters are traced with his own fine pen. Every man to his own methods, but M. Poincaré's readers, and especially his printers, have perhaps sometimes longed for some slight abatement of this special instance of ministerial industry. Legibility, by the by—or rather alleged illegibility—is a point on which men and women, especially those in the winter of life, are apt to be touchy. In the last year of his long life the Duke of Wellington sent to Lord Derby a note which no one in Downing Street could decipher. Colonel Talbot, the private secretary, hurried to Apsley House to ask the Duke to explain his own letter. The reply, accompanied by a smile, was prompt, if unhelpful. " It was *my* business to write that letter, but it is *your* duty to read it."

The most prolific and conscientious letter-writer of the last quarter of a century was Lord Curzon. No subject was too trivial, none too large—provided it interested him—for his correct, courteous, and sometimes rather flamboyant pen. There was apparently no conscious attempt, in the dozens of letters which he daily dashed off, to polish a sentence or round off a suggestion ; but it was as impossible for him, whatever his hurry, to make any error in his prose, as it would be for Paderewski, whatever the circumstances, to play a false note. No man, perhaps, subscribed more heartily than Lord Curzon to the dictum of Locke in delicate allusion to Sir William Temple : " The writing of letters enters so much into all occasions of life that no gentleman can avoid showing himself in composition of this kind. Occurrences will daily force him to make this use of his pen, which lays open his breeding, his sense, and his abilities, to a severer examination than any oral discourse."

Among modern letter-writers, Mr. Gladstone towers high ; with him earnest, inexhaustible, infinite, the pen was no instrument of diversion. Nor, indeed, will his masterpieces much divert the ordinary reader. In times of religious or political storm he would further darken the sky with his post cards, but his letters alone must have chained him, especially when out of office, to his desk for hours at a time. Their length was inordinate, their depth sometimes such that the ordinary reader would be quickly out of his own. " My dear Manning," he writes to the future pre-eminent Cardinal in 1887, " I gladly appropriate a peaceful hour for renewing the consideration of the great subjects to which your two letters refer." The conception of a " peaceful hour " no doubt varies. Mr. Gladstone's notion, at the age of seventy-seven, was to draft an epistle containing over 3,000 words, in which arguments are as closely woven as they are elaborately embroidered, where Church establishments, the sons of Sciva, reservation of truth, and scriptural influences lead up to the solemn declaration that " the road from separation of Church and State to Atheism is, if indirect, yet broad and open."

Mr. Gladstone's correspondence passes human belief, and almost transcends its endurance ; his range was far wider than Lord Curzon's or perhaps that of any other statesman within knowledge ; he was not only punctual in reply, but he was at no sensible pains to spare himself from opening up a correspondence to which it would be difficult to set a term. The fire-proof room which he built at Hawarden contains sixty thousand " selected letters," with tens of thousands more to which that dignified epithet could not be applied. Six hundred holographs from Queen Victoria figure in the former category. The letters are, for the most part, long, with the exception of Lord Granville's, who was always as brief as possible on paper. Yet Mr. Gladstone could tell him that his letters weighed fifteen pounds and a half. As opposite numbers to this mass of " letters in " there are more than a score and a half of huge folios containing copies of his " letters out." Mr. Gladstone, when he believed the motives of those who addressed him to be sincere, spared neither time nor trouble nor stationery in his answer. He could not indeed say : *Semper ego auditor tantum ?* but that was in fact the spirit behind the man. Yet now and again his patience is strained. A well-known Evangelical lady writes about " turbulence in Ireland," which she attributes to his inaction, to unprincipled colleagues, and to want of heavenly guidance. The reply, though perfectly courteous, is on a par with Father Stanton's answer to the lady who thought her cook had " Roman Catholic tendencies," and would he come and talk to her ? " Madam, if your cook is really a good one, I advise you to look leniently at the Roman Catholic tendencies."

Mr. Gladstone's letters, with all their literary merit, all their devastating earnestness, bear a strong family resemblance to one another ; nor at any time could it be said of them, as was said of Cardinal Newman's, that they are instinct with the consciousness of the person he addresses. The great Liberal Prime Minister's letters are read—and there is evidence that they are not yet on the dusty shelf of neglect—for what he has to say. Lord Beaconsfield's letters have been eagerly pounced upon, not for what that spectacular genius had to say, but for the opulent way in which he said it. How often does one open a book in which the author, in the course of a rather forced preface, assures us that the contents were never intended to see the light of day ; that no one was more surprised, no one more reluctant than himself, when his literary advisers urged publication.

> "At friends' request my works have seen the day ;
> Deuce take those friends, is all that I can say !"

The real test of letter-writing, as of story-telling, is whether the writer has really something to say to his or her correspondent ; whether the letter springs from the heart, or must be affiliated upon the ink-pot. Who, I wonder, was that memorable person to whom the first letter of all must be ascribed ? Credit for this diverting innovation has been given to that Persian princess who became the mother of Xerxes. A famous Doctor of Divinity has, however, assured us that centuries before there existed a man (or a syndicate) called Homer, one Panbesa wrote to one Amenomapt, praising with discriminating eulogy the delectable city of Rameses. According to this old-world Egyptian gentleman, nothing in the Theban land could compare with Rameses, where vine and fig-tree flourished, where nursery gardens laughed in the sun, where wine and cider and beer were as gaily drunk as they were bountifully produced.

Letter-writing can perhaps trace its genesis to a hankering or hunger for sympathy. Primæval man, we may be sure, cared little for what his neighbours thought, and certainly would not be at the trouble to direct those thoughts into any particular channel. Civilisation is responsible for the desire to circulate our sentiment, report our doings, inquire curiously as to those of our friends, and press our opinions on one another. And vanity too has counted a great deal.

Exhuming slightly the past, one remembers how few letters are to be found in the Old Testament, and that the writers of these are people on a higher

social level than the Israelites. One must look
Romeward for specimens of early letter-writing,
and especially for the sort of letters which either
deal with domestic matters or are apt nowadays
to be marked—if not treated—as confidential.
Cicero—one of the earliest types of the public
man who is always occupied but never hurried,
who is as acceptable as he is active, and who can
always find time to do things because he never
tried to do two things at a time—was surely a
natural letter-writer. If he can be charged with
a little affectation in his other writings, he was
simplicity itself when addressing his friends. He
never sat down, as did Mme de Sévigné or
Horace Walpole, with half an eye on the person
addressed, and an eye and a half on the public for
whom the words were really intended. M. Boissier,
in his *Cicéron et ses Amis*, compares the letters of
the Roman scribe with those of Mme de Sévigné.
The compliment to his gifted compatriot was the
highest he could bestow, though Ste. Beuve's was
the more subtle flattery, when, on a wet day in a
country house, he suggested : " *Lisons tous Mme
de Sévigné.*" Perhaps no two talented writers
were ever wider apart. The correspondence of
Cicero is almost as full of meat as Bacon's essays ;
the Frenchwoman produced literary soufflés in

which the material counted for little, the flavour and the lightness being the triumphant merits of her literary cuisine.

The champions of Cicero *contra mundum* denounce Pliny as a prig, whose priggishness coloured what he wrote no less than what he said and did. Pliny was anyhow that dreadful thing—a boy prodigy; he wrote a tragedy when he was only fourteen. And then at seventeen, during the great eruption of Vesuvius, while his uncle is being asphyxiated and his mother is in paroxysms of panic, he calls for a volume of Livy and makes extracts as if nothing were happening. Was this youthful heroism, or " playing to the gallery " ? Pliny's writings—and he could beyond question write—are plainly pervaded by the impression that posterity ought to be devilish grateful to him for so kindly writing at all. He was, however, rich, and riches sometimes clog the pen. Aurelius Symmachus was even richer, so rich that he, or his sons, could afford to let the public read his letters ; yet here we find the first instance of that now daily, if not hourly test, the begging letter. Is it, or is it not, true that a generation later Sidonius Apollinaris took Symmachus for his model ? One wonders who started that hare, for the pupil was curiously unlike his supposed master. The style of the one is as flimsy as that of the other is solid. A child could see through the one ; it takes a student, and one who does not mind ugliness, to appreciate at whatever is its full worth, the other. You might as well compare Mrs. Hemans with Walt Whitman.

Experts in Hagiology point to the bundles of letters for which St. Augustine, St. Jerome, St. Basil, and St. Francis of Sales are responsible— those of the last named being marked by a literary charm, if not a literary quality, scarcely attained by the others. St. Augustine's letters are for the most part religious treatises of a tiresome character dealing with matters of theology or philosophy ; they are adorned with little grace and less warmth, except in the single instance where he thanks a young lady for sending him a tunic which she had woven for her dead brother. Dr. Jessop has been forward to remind us that St. Jerome's 150 letters are for the most part unpractical ; chiefly valuable for the notices of contemporary religious life and interesting for the impression they leave of the high pressure at which devout people were living at the end of the fourth century. One letter, however, contains injunctions which might well be delivered from a West-End pulpit to-day. The lady addressed—obviously youthful

—is not to mince her words as the fashion then was (clip them, we should say to-day) ; she is not to paint or to have her ears bored ; she is not to dye her hair red, or allow any young gentlemen with curly hair to smile at her.

St. Basil's letters, of which about 400 have come down to us, are far more succulent morsels, not only on account of their style, but because their range of subject is much wider, and because St. Basil's correspondents are drawn from all ranks and classes, from all sorts and conditions of men. But one's heart sinks to remember that the saint himself, who is associated with all that is beautiful, both in human and canine life, when he came to office, sank the abbot in the man. His neighbour steals his pigs ; he does not invite him to return them, but threatens that if he does not, " I will beyond doubt excommunicate thee for thine evil doings."

It is a commonplace of the barrack square that pickled. red cabbage is a wonderful restorative after unwise potation. St. Basil was a convert to pickled cabbage, though I suppose for different reasons. " My dear Sir," he writes to the Governor of Cappadocia, " I never believed in cabbage before ; still less in pickled cabbage ; but now I shall praise it as something superior to the lotus

Homer talks of, yea, not inferior to the very ambrosia served as food to the gods." So across the centuries good St. Basil touches hands with the lighter-hearted of our gallant defenders.

It has been said—I am neither bold enough to assent nor to deny—that for more than a thousand years the art of free and fresh letter-writing was dormant or even defunct. The letters which swarm in mediæval literature would be more suitably dubbed epistles; what they possess in dignity, they for the most part lose in charm; they are official in tone if not in text, impersonal in character, and circumscribed in outlook.

In the fifteenth and early sixteenth centuries we come upon the collection known as the Paston Letters, addressed to one another by members of a highly placed family between 1422 and 1509.

When Mr. Herman Merivale sought—and happily failed—to impugn their authenticity, he argued that their style was infinitely more simple than other publications of that period. His statement was just; his inference wrong. The Paston Letters now reposing in the National Archives are models of all that easy and familiar letters—in the right sense of the adjectives—

I—4

should be, whereas contemporary works were too often monuments of infelicitous writing, of wordy phrases and windy protests, of commonplaces disguised by a thick sauce of attempted fine writing—the sort of fine writing which, odious in a book, is intolerable in a letter.

The Paston Letters, despite their intimacy—the intimacy born of close family ties—more than fulfil one of the best and most useful purposes. They throw a strong sidelight on the perturbed state of national affairs ; they show the nobles living in a state of civil war ; they illustrate vividly the course of public events, as well as the manners and morals of the moment.

They yield indeed in avoirdupois to the mammoth series of papers which have their home at Hatfield, but *qua* personal letters require some research to find their superiors, and some boldness to proclaim them. The Cecil correspondence, said to contain upwards of 30,000 documents, goes to swell the huge assemblage of letters which can be attributed to the seventeenth century ; their quantity is prodigious ; their quality more doubtful, perhaps because they are under the same sort of constraint which marked the scanty output of letters under the Commonwealth, a constraint from which there was recovery when James II came to the throne, and emancipation after the accession of Anne.

If letter-writing is to be judged in any degree by results, Lord Chesterfield, the exemplar of manners and elegance, must be reckoned a failure. Day in, day out, year in and year out, he drenched both his natural son and his godson with advisory, if not minatory, epistles, in which good manners rather, perhaps, than good morals are enjoined as the goal of endeavour. Yet the natural son was always a lout, while Fanny Burney—who knew what she was talking about—pronounced the godson to have " as little good reading as any man I ever met with."

" I quite agree with you as to the horrors of correspondence. Correspondence is like small clothes before the invention of suspenders ; it was impossible to keep them up." So thought Sydney Smith, and just at a moment, too, when such correspondence as passed between Gray and Walpole, or between Gray and Mason, may have been fresh in his mind. It has been well said that Pope and Bolingbroke wrote for fame, Gray and Horace Walpole for love of it. Gray's letters are finished, though never laboured, compositions ; Walpole wrote from sheer lust of writing ; it was pure *cacoethes*; he would have written wherever he was ; and in whatever circumstances, even if no means—no post or messenger—had been available to make public what he wrote. " Office," once said Lord Rosebery, " is indeed an acquired taste, though by habit persons may learn to relish it, just as men learn to love absinthe or opium or cod-liver oil." Walpole's love of expressing himself on paper was the very reverse of an acquired taste ; it was born in him, or rather burnt into him at his birth. Had Walpole any superior in later days as a letter-writer ? The answer to such a question would of course be a shout of Charles Lamb, and the shout would be echoed far and wide, and with warrant. Walpole's letters were golden, but there was alloy in them ; Charles Lamb's were the pure metal. One was as affected as the other was sincere. There is a certain knowledge that Lamb was immune from the assaults of jealousy or revenge ; only once was he obviously hurt, when Southey unintentionally jagged an old wound. There is laughter on Charles Lamb's lips, and humour streams from his pen ; but no laughter at the thrust of a barbed weapon, or the double meaning of an indecorous jest. He could never have laughed at a joke unlovely or unkind, simply because it would have been no joke to him at all.

Of women letter-writers it is reasonable to glance at Lady Mary Wortley Montagu in the seventeenth, and Mrs. Carlyle in the eighteenth century. Lady Mary's letters won a swift fame ; and her quarrel with Pope—due, it is always suggested, to Pope having lent the Montagus a pair of sheets which they failed to return—did nothing to lessen her *réclame*. Lady Mary's classical education and rather masculine leanings—as masculine leanings were appraised in her day—did much to advance, nothing to mar, the value of her correspondence. She had every merit except one which is so often denied to women writers, a sense of humour. Her descriptions of scenery—how crushingly boring is the ordinary scribe's description of scenery !—are of a piece with her stories of men and women, her criticism of local custom ; no pen was ever more fluent ; yet so carefully built up was what she wrote that to extract a sentence would be like removing a brick from a very concentrated building. Mrs. Carlyle's letters were never intended—really never intended—for the public eye ; had they been, she would surely have taken care to add the modicum of sugar which would have corrected the bitter taste so often left in her reader's mouth. Her letters are acid, but never insipid ; nothing escapes her uncanny power of observation ; and she was at little pains to dress up in pretty clothes what she wanted to say, what perhaps she could not help saying. Yet for sheer beauty, for haunting pathos, it would be difficult to surpass her narrative of that solitary visit to Haddington after her father's death.

And another volume lies before me to which I must refer. Queen Victoria's letters are judged, and will be judged by posterity, not for their loose grammar and faulty construction ; nor for the indifferent usage of the first and third person ; not even for the fresh knowledge which we derive of the actors in the Victorian drama ; her letters serve to lift, perhaps a little abruptly, the veil from a great Sovereign who reigned in something like mystery as well as majesty, to show with what tenacious grip one small, capable hand gripped the prerogative of a crown, while the other held the threads of Empire ; to show too that it was still possible for a constitutional monarch— without ever outstepping the Constitution—to control and at times override her Ministers.

There is one phase of letter-writing which seemingly is enjoying a daily growth. To the novel-reader of fifty years ago there was nothing grotesque in the passionate sobs which shook the frame of "A Maiden of our own Day," when with streaming eyes and bowed head she admitted to her grandmother that she had written to the *Times* newspaper to applaud Mr. Gladstone's championship of Greek liberty. The maiden of this day might not consider the *Times* as the most suitable vehicle for carrying her views, but she would have little hesitation in communicating with the Press, even on subjects which might more appropriately lie within the province of a matron.

II

I have more than once heard the question put : Who is the best English letter-writer ? The answer has always depended on the taste of the person addressed. Mr. E. V. Lucas once put the question to himself, and made the observation upon it that " it is a mistake when a letter-writer is a man of action with too much to tell. He is then in danger of becoming exciting. The best letter-writers never excite : they entertain, amuse, interest, excite never. A humorous observer of life, of strong affections, and possessed of sufficient egotism to desire to keep his friends acquainted with his thoughts, adventures, moods, and achievements, is, when he is without responsibilities or harassing demands on his time, in the ideal position to write such letters as become literature." Mr. Lucas has perhaps never realised how personal, how egotistical (in the better sense) is this criticism. It describes exactly what I judge to be his own attitude towards life, his own demands from—and contributions to—literature.

He chooses Cowper, FitzGerald, Gray, and Walpole as letter-writers who fulfil his conditions. I have already referred to Gray and Walpole ; FitzGerald is not a letter-writer whom I greatly enjoy ; but for Cowper I can largely share Mr. Lucas's enthusiasm. I like most Cowper's humour, as in that pleasant letter wherein he consoles a friend who is staying at Ramsgate but would rather be at Margate :

" When I was at Margate, it was an excursion of pleasure to go to see Ramsgate. The pier, I remember, was accounted a most excellent piece of stone-work, and such I found it. By this time, I suppose, it is finished ; and surely it is no small advantage, that you have an opportunity of observing how nicely these great stones are put together, as often as you please, without either trouble or expense. But you think Margate more lively. So is a Cheshire cheese full of mites more lively than a sound one : but that very liveliness only proves its rottenness. I remember, too, that

Margate, though full of company, was generally filled with such company, as people who were nice in the choice of their company, were rather fearful of keeping company with. The hoy went to London every week, loaded with mackerel and herrings, and returned loaded with company. The cheapness of the conveyance made it equally commodious for Dead fish and Lively company. So, perhaps, your solitude at Ramsgate may turn out another advantage ; at least I should think it one."

And I recall too that other and more serious letter of consolation that he sent to a woman-friend under a cloud of misfortune :

" I would give you, Madam, not my counsel only, but consolation also, were I not disqualified from that delightful service by a great dearth of it in my own experience. I, too, often seek but cannot find it. . . .

" I was much struck by an expression in your letter to Hayley where you say that ' you will endeavour to take an interest in green leaves again.' This seems the sound of my own voice reflected to me from a distance ; I have so often had the same thought and desire.

"A day scarcely passes at this season of the year when I do not contemplate the trees so soon to be stript, and say, perhaps I shall never see you clothed again ; every year as it passes makes this expectation more reasonable, and the year, with me, cannot be very distant when the event will verify it. Well—may God grant us a good hope of arriving in due time where the leaves never fall, and all will be right."

Byron's letters are, I must admit, with all their insolence, much more to my taste than the delicate insipidity of the recluse of Olney. Unlike Mr. Lucas, I am clearly of opinion that a spice of " excitement " gives a savour to a letter. One of Byron's letters to Sir Walter Scott is surely to be classed among the best :

" I have lately had some anxiety, rather than trouble, about an awkward affair here, which you may perhaps have heard of ; but our minister has behaved very handsomely, and the Tuscan Government as well as it is possible for such a government to behave, which is not saying much for the latter. Some other English, and Scots, and myself had a brawl with a dragoon, who insulted one of the party, and whom we mistook for an officer, as he was medalled and well-mounted, etc. ; but he turned out to be a serjeant-major. He called out the guard at the gates to arrest us (we being unarmed) ; upon which I and another (an Italian) rode through the said guard ; but they succeeded in detaining others of the party. I rode to my house, and sent my secretary to give an account of the attempted and illegal arrest to the authorities, and then, without dismounting, rode back towards the gates, which are near my present mansion. Half-way I met my man vapouring away and threatening to draw upon me (who had a cane in my hand, and no other arms). I, still believing him an officer, demanded his name and address, and gave him my hand and glove thereupon. A servant of mine thrust in between us (totally without orders), but let him go on my command. He then rode off at full speed ; but about forty paces further was stabbed, and very dangerously (so as to be in peril), by some *Callum Beg* or other of my people (for I have some rough-handed folks about me), I need hardly say without my direction or approval. The said dragoon had been sabring our unarmed countrymen, however, at the *gate, after they were in arrest,* and held by the guards, and wounded one, Captain Hay, very severely. However, he got his paiks—having acted like an assassin, and being treated like one. *Who* wounded him, though it was done before thousands of people, they have never been able to ascertain, or prove, nor even the *weapon* ; some said a *pistol,* an *air-gun,* a stiletto, a sword, a lance, a pitchfork, and what not. They have arrested and examined servants and people of all descriptions, but can make out nothing. Mr. Dawkins, our minister, assures me that no suspicion is entertained of the man who wounded him having been instigated by me, or any of the party. I enclose you copies of the depositions of those with us, and Dr. Crau-furd, a canny Scot (*not* an acquaintance), who saw the latter part of the affair."

Of Byron's love-letters few surpass the one he wrote to the Marchesa Guiccioli in a copy of *Corinne*. As a writer of love-letters he was just about as reliable as Burns. And he had a certain finesse which the other lacked. Byron wrote this particular letter in the lady's garden when she was away; for he used to make his morning call in her absence as when she was there:

" MY DEAREST TERESA,—I have read this book in your garden;—my love, you were absent, or else I could not have read it. It is a favourite book of yours, and the writer was a friend of mine. You will not understand these English words, and others will not understand them—which is the reason I have not scrawled them in Italian. But you will recognise the handwriting of him who passionately loved you, and you will divine that, over a book which was yours, he could only think of love. In that word, beautiful in all languages, but most so in yours—Amor mio—is comprised my existence here and hereafter. I feel I exist here, and I fear that I shall exist hereafter,—to what purpose you will decide; my destiny rests with you, and you are a woman, eighteen years of age, and two out of a convent. I wish that you had stayed there, with all my heart—or, at least, that I had never met you in your married state.

" But all this is too late. I love you, and you love me,—at least, you say so, and act as if you did so, which last is a great consolation in all events. But I more than love you, and cannot cease to love you.

" Think of me sometimes, when the Alps and the ocean divide us,—but they never will, unless you wish it."

Of my other favourites, Burns's letters are remarkable, not merely for their charm, which is great, but for the number and variety of the correspondents to whom they are addressed. No fewer than one hundred and fifty people share reception of the few hundred letters that survive, which are but a part of what he actually wrote. As the recipients were in every walk of life, it follows that Burns's letters are a mine of interest. The style is as varied as the subject. Take for example the exalted letter which he sent to Miss Alexander with a poem. I quote the first half of it :

" MADAM,—Poets are such *outré* beings, so much the children of wayward fancy and capricious whim, that I believe the world generally allows them a larger latitude in the laws of propriety than the sober sons of judgment and prudence. I mention this as an apology for the liberties that a nameless stranger has taken with you in the inclosed poem, which he begs leave to present you with. Whether it has poetical merit any way worthy of the theme, I am not the proper judge : but it is the best my abilities can produce ; and what to a good heart will, perhaps, be a superior grace, it is equally sincere as fervent.

" The scenery was nearly taken from real life, though I dare say, Madam, you do not recollect it, as I believe you scarcely noticed the poetic *rêveur* as he wandered by you. I had roved out as chance directed, in the favourite haunts of my muse, on the banks of the Ayr, to view nature in all the gaiety of the vernal year. The evening sun was flaming over the distant western hills ; not a breath stirred the crimson opening blossom, or the verdant spreading leaf. It was a golden moment for a poetic heart. I listened to the feathered warblers, pouring their harmony on every hand, with a congenial kindred regard, and frequently turned out of my path, lest I should disturb their little songs, or frighten them to another station. Surely, said I to myself, he must be a wretch indeed, who, regardless of your harmonious endeavour to please him, can eye your elusive flights to discover your secret recesses, and to rob you of all the property nature gives you—your dearest comforts, your helpless nest-lings."

" Had Calumny and Villainy taken my walk," he continues, " they had at that moment sworn eternal peace " with the lady he addresses. Six years later he added a postscript, on quite a different note :

" Well, Mr. Burns, and *did* the lady give you the desired permission ? No ; she was too fine a lady to *notice* so plain a compliment. As to her great brothers whom I have met since in life on more equal terms of respectability—why should I quarrel with their want of attention to me ? When fate swore that their purses should be full, nature was equally positive that their heads should be empty. Men of their fashion were surely incapable of being unpolite ? Ye canna mak' a silk-purse o' a sow's lug."

I should become tedious if I were with elaborate argument to examine closely the claims of those letter-writers whom on the whole I place highest. But it might be well, if only by way of contrast, to consider one or two letters which were not written with the object, dear to Mr. Lucas, of " entertaining and amusing " the recipient. The subject of *Irritating and Displeasing Letters* would provide the theme of an admirable essay. I shall not attempt it here, but what thoughts on letter-writing can be complete without mention of Dr. Johnson's immortal rebuke to Lord Chesterfield, the greatest epistle of all time ? It is too familiar to quote in full, but I cannot deprive myself of the pleasure, the almost physical pleasure, of tracing some of those sonorous periods in my own hand :

" Seven years, my Lord, have now past, since I waited in your outward rooms, or was repulsed from your door ; during which time I have been pushing on my work through difficulties, of which it is useless to complain, and have brought it at last, to the verge of publication, without one act of assistance, one word of encouragement, or one smile of favour. Such treatment I did not expect, for I never had a Patron before. The shepherd in Virgil grew at last acquainted with Love, and found him a native of the rocks.

" Is not a Patron, my Lord, one who looks with unconcern on a man struggling for life in the water, and when he has reached ground, encumbers him with help ? The notice which you have been pleased to take of my labours, had it been early, had been kind ; but it has been delayed till I am indifferent, and cannot enjoy it ; till I am solitary, and cannot impart it ; till I am known, and do not want it. I hope it is no very cynical asperity not to confess obligations where no benefit has been received, or to be unwilling that the publick should consider me as owing that to a Patron, which Providence has enabled me to do for myself."

And since I am ending this branch of my essay on a more serious note, there is a letter written by a master of English prose, which to my mind is the saddest message ever sent by one human being to another. It was written by Swift, to

Mrs. Whiteway, his niece, when he felt the shades of death—a living death worse than any natural end—falling over him :

" I have been very miserable all night, and to-day extremely deaf and full of pain. I am so stupid and confounded that I cannot express the mortification I am under both of body and mind. All I can say is that I am not in torture ; but I daily and hourly expect it. Pray let me know how your health is and your family : I hardly understand one word I write. I am sure my days will be very few ; few and miserable they must be. I am, for those few days, yours entirely,
Jonathan Swift.

" If I do not blunder, it is Saturday, July 26, 1740.
" If I live till Monday, I shall hope to see you, perhaps for the last time."

When one reads this heart-breaking cry of stricken genius, Mr. Lucas's desire to be amused, interested, but never excited seems natural, but rather superficial.

III

An occasional love-letter has been referred to in the earlier part of this paper, but no attempt has been made to examine this interesting branch

I—5

of correspondence in any general fashion. Love-letters must on the whole be admitted to be extremely boring. But a distinction may, of course, be drawn. When two people love one another their letters are, naturally, to one another, divine. They write simply, lovingly, without sophistication. But I do not mean that kind of love-letter ; I mean the letter which is intended to live ; which is written to harness passion to the chariot of literary immortality. In other words, I mean an affectation.

Such letters, in my opinion, almost invariably fail. For the letters of " true love," in the Scottish phrase, must be simple and spontaneous. Nothing studied or artificial can live in that sweet and simple atmosphere. They exist for two people and for two only. How happy while it lasts !

Only the love-letters of distinguished people are in the end published. (I pass over the ephemeral revelations of the law courts in divorce or breach-of-promise cases.) The fact that they are published in numbers so disturbingly great should surely establish *in limine* a grave caution, which indeed may almost be expressed in the form of an established aphorism. It might be defined as follows :

Every distinguished man who writes passionate

love-letters may be quite sure that one day they will be published. Nearly every distinguished woman in the same case may expect the same result.

The plague of the matter is that such letters are always kept by a woman *unless they are deeply compromising to herself*. A man, half Lothario, half Machiavelli, might usefully notice the excepted case.

I do not for a moment believe that Lord Beaconsfield's rather absurd, rather pompous, letters to Lady Bradford and others—written sometimes from the dullness of a Victorian Cabinet—were ever intended to be read by the world. But if men of brilliant quality and achievement write letters of love, or even of dilettante attraction, to women who like them, it is almost certain that those who receive them will never destroy them. Often they themselves would never dream of publishing them. But when Death the Surpriser deals his swift blow, such letters are always available for the executor. *He* will probably not publish them ; but they will not be destroyed. They swell the family heirloom of valued trifles until, in one generation or two, there arises a member of the family who discerns and exploits this sidelight upon a great man's life. Evidently no one would publish an absolutely banal love-letter—no one, I ought to add, except Mrs. O'Shea. And accordingly most of the Love-letters of the Great which have survived suggest the midnight oil and indicate the hope of immortality.

Nothing but extreme literary genius can make a love-letter live. Why should it ? It is nearly always stilted, exaggerated, and stereotyped in idea. It deals with dead ones. Only genius can recapture its beauty. And even so egotism will probably by exaggerating disfigure it. What sensible woman, however intelligent, if really in love, would care a brass farthing for the sort of stuff we are indulged with in the anthologies of amorous correspondence ? She would sell them all for a short and sweet assurance. She knows herself ; she knows the male exaggeration of herself. The heroines of Ovid, to be sure, wrote quite musical and rather moving letters ; but we must remember that they had all been deserted. A true love-letter must, by the terms of the game, be exchanged between people who still love one another.

On the whole I admit that I find these disinterred romances tiresome ; but here and there a phrase lives. Napoleon writes from Italy to Josephine (who had already other distractions) : " I have your letter, my admirable love. It has

filled my heart with joy. Since I left you I have
been sad all the time. My only happiness is near
you. I go over endlessly in my thoughts your
kisses, your tears, your endless jealousy. Ah,
when shall I be able to pass every minute near you,
with nothing to do but love you ; and nothing to
think of but the pleasure of telling you, and of
proving it ? . . . Ah, let me see some of your faults ;
be less beautiful, less graceful, less tender, less
good. But never be jealous and never shed tears.
Your tears send me out of my mind ; they set
my very blood on fire."

The value (and it is considerable) of these burning words is perhaps a little diminished by the
subsequent history of the correspondents. What
idolatry (one is tempted to add) and what folly !
Nor is a similar observation unreasonable in
relation to the charming poems which He of the
" Magic Casements " wrote to Her who was
unromantically christened Brawne. The verses
would have been so delicious if we had not known
what happened afterwards. And it is after all
rather tiresome to be told by a man of genius
that a certain lady was wonderful and charming
when you clearly realise (and he afterwards
found out) that she was nothing of the kind.
How ironic now the dead words which this

poet of charm and fantasy addressed to his
Brawne :

" You fear sometimes that I do not love you
so much as you wish. My dear girl, I love you
for ever and ever and without reserve. The more
I have known, the more I have loved. In every
way—even my jealousies have been agonies of
love—in the hottest fit I would have died for
you. I have vexed you too much. But for love !
Can I help it ? You are always new. The last of
your kisses was ever the sweetest ; the last smile
the brightest ; the last movement the grace-
fullest."

That such a man should have loved such a woman
in such a way contributes only one item to that
ironical history of sex problems which will never
be completely solved.

Napoleon and Nelson were in reality the supreme
protagonists of a great world-struggle. Napoleon
(for a short time) was very stupid about Josephine ;
Nelson, far more profoundly, and for an unending
period, about that super-woman who out-Phryned
Phryne. Nor was Wellington immune, even in
quite important moments, from feminine attraction. And yet Napoleon, Wellington, and Nelson
were incomparably the greatest men of action
who between them determined certainly the

destinies of a continent, and perhaps the future of the world. All these men were incredibly virile. Each was responsive (except where the road of professional duty clearly lay elsewhere) to feminine influence. At that supreme moment in the world's history women had not the vote ; could they want more than they had then ? It is probably true that nearly all great men (unless they suffer from disability) react to the influence, and profit by the friendship, of some member of the other sex. But they would on the whole, I think, be wise to be economic in their love-letters.

It should certainly be placed on record, lest it should be supposed that romantic, or even irregular, attachments had been the principal subject-matter of this essay, that one of the most charming love-letters on record was written by a comparatively old husband to a comparatively old wife. The author was Nathaniel Hawthorne :

" I am sometimes driven to wish that you and I could mount upon a cloud and be borne quite out of sight and hearing of the world ; for now all the people in the world seem to come between us. How happy were Adam and Eve ! We love one another as well as they ; but there is no silent and lovely garden of Eden for us. Will you sail away with me to discover some summer island ? Do you not think that God has reserved one for us ever since the beginning of the world ? "

If I were to answer this last question cynically, I should say that in my opinion it was most unlikely, or, at the most hopeful prognosis, that the couple were fortunate. The dream is, however, charming.

But we are, after all, engaged in a deeper inquiry, upon which I have the hardihood to proclaim and make known to the world a more definite conclusion. It is capable of statement in these propositions :

1. No love is worth loving which would not repel and even be affronted by its public advertisement.

2. No true lover could ever write a line in sincerity to the woman whom he loves which he would now or hereafter have published to the world.

3. The storied loves of the world have only conquered romance, and invaded legend, because they were never realised or tested upon the terms of domestic co-partnership.

And I will not recant these views until the voice of ultimate Truth informs me what would have happened in the fifth year of the marriage of Dante and Beatrice. Personally, I think that they started too high and that their ideals would have declined ; perhaps even the superb genius of his poetry would have ceased to attract. We have no reason for supposing that Beatrice enjoyed poetry. Most beautiful women do not.

III

SIR WALTER SCOTT

MY Lord Provost, my Lords, ladies and gentlemen, I must, I think, justify my presence here [1] at the outset by making one practical observation such as I hope may be heard with patience by Scots. The Society over which I preside to-night is one which reflects credit upon that fidelity to the great men of the past which has for long distinguished your folk. It is, believe me, a society which deserves the support of the citizens of Edinburgh, and I hope, occupying the position of President, that I may be allowed to urge upon those here to-night, in the happy capacity of irresponsible guests, that they should hasten to become members of the Society, and by doing so both reinforce its finances and contribute some further distinction to the memory of the greatest of Scottish writers, who had also some larger claims of which I will speak hereafter.

When I was asked to become President of a

[1] This address was delivered to the Scott Society in Edinburgh on Friday, December 5, 1924.

club which is already ancient, I accepted the
invitation, as was indeed natural, but not without
trepidation, for it seemed to me that this club
must from the very nature of the case consist
mainly of Scots, and that he who presides over
such a club should naturally and normally be a
Scot ; but I corrected a view which was perhaps
somewhat timidly formed by recalling a remark
which your old friend and admirer Dr. Johnson
made in reply to one who was putting the prerogative of the Crown very high. The line was
quoted, " Who rules o'er freemen should himself
be free " ; Dr. Johnson said, " Sir, I cannot agree
with you. It might as well be said : ' Who
drives fat oxen should himself be fat.' " So I
was led to believe, encouraged by your considered
invitation, that he who leads Scottish admirers
of Sir Walter Scott might, at least for the period
of twelve months, be permitted to be an Englishman.

My incapacity for the task could not be more
plainly exhibited than by the fact that I was
constrained to-night to refuse even perfunctory
tribute to the noble national dish which graced
your table ; but, on the other hand, I may claim
what I think few in this room can assert, that,
before I went to Oxford more than thirty years

ago, I had read every one of Scott's novels at least three times ; and I do not believe that one quinquennium has passed without my re-reading them all within the period. And I can make the further claim that, without ever having been supported by any resource of wealth, having always to consider and reconsider any extravagance at the bookseller's, I possess to-day a first edition of all Scott's poems and a first edition of all Scott's novels, including the rare " Waverley," though not, unhappily, clad in its original boards.

And indeed it would be a view very incomplete of the genius of that revered figure, whom to-night we celebrate, if it were to be supposed that he was only a Scottish hero. It is a common experience that English politicians or public men who address Scottish audiences are corrected for too frequent a reference to a not unworthy, but an incomplete adjective—I mean the word " English." I may, perhaps, retort upon this occasion that to claim Scott as purely Scottish would be doing a wrong to the memory of a very versatile and most complete citizen of the Empire. When I look back upon his career, upon his teaching, upon the inspiration which he has breathed for so many years into the youth of the Empire, I

think of him rather as a great Briton. I recall
that over a period of years charged with crisis,
not only to the fortunes of Scotland, but to the
fortunes of that Empire in which Scotland is a
shining unit, there was none more eloquent, none
more untiring, in his presentation of the national
case against the tyranny of the Napoleonic system
than Walter Scott.

Nor were the reverberations and the reactions
of his message confined to this country of Scotland. They found readers and made converts the
whole world over. Congruously, therefore, with
the teachings of which he was the eloquent, and
at times almost the inspired mouthpiece, I recall
the lines which thrilled not only Scotland but
England when the astonishing career of the
younger Pitt was prematurely closed :

> " The trumpet's silver sound is still,
> The Warden silent on the hill."

We look back, as we must so many years after
his death, in cool, passionless review over the
career of a great man of letters. It is sometimes
helpful, it is sometimes reasonable, to examine
him who is the subject of your thought as a man
as well as a writer ; sometimes (though not
always) it is even kinder. The shades, the phan-

toms of François Villon, Benvenuto Cellini, Byron,
and Oscar Wilde are entitled to urge that they
should be considered, and should be considered
mainly, as artists by posterity. The claim is
fairly well founded, though Byron could make a
distinguishable case. When a human being has
contributed something of genius, something permanent and vital, to human thought and to human
art, he is entitled to claim that the generations
which follow shall extirpate from their minds
recollections, however grave and painful, of any
human infirmity which may have disfigured his
career. For art is one thing and morals quite
another. The contribution of the artist is not to be
disparaged by the recollection or the arraignment
of ethical frailty. But when we deal, as it is our
happiness to deal to-night, with one whose life
and example were as pure and as admirable as
were those of Walter Scott, it is reasonable to begin
the attempt to understand what he was, and what
he stood for, by some appraisement, however
slightly attempted, of his qualities as a man.

I do not know—and I choose my words carefully, not applying them without earlier reflection
—I do not know of the career of any great man
of letters more consistent, simpler, nobler, braver,
than the career of Walter Scott. It made, inevi-

tably made, when once the brilliancy of his literary equipment was realised, a strong and lasting appeal to the loyalty and admiration of the Scottish people. In every bone, in every fibre of his inmost being, he was Scottish. He was sprung from the loins of men who had ridden hotly in many a mad foray, in many a bloody raid. I cannot doubt that had he been free to determine his own career, had he not suffered almost from childhood from depressing physical ailments, he would have wished for himself, responding to the blood that flowed through his veins, the career of a man of action or, as he might have said, of *derring do*.

You have been reminded to-night of the words in which that great soldier, Wolfe, stated at a supreme moment of his career—one of the great moments in history, a moment which was to determine the future of the British Empire, perhaps even the civilisation of the western continents—that he would rather have written the noble words of Gray's " Elegy " than have stormed Quebec. To me it seems on the whole probable that, approaching such a choice from an inverted angle, Scott would have sacrificed the whole of his poetry, the whole of the Waverley novels, could he have stood, a Scottish soldier, in one of those squares at Waterloo which faced unconquered and unconquerable the bitter succession of French assaults.

As I look back upon that kindly and meritorious life (for I am talking of him at this moment not in relation to his literary quality, but as a Scottish citizen and Scottish gentleman), I like to think of him (and to me this may be conceded as a Scots lawyer of late admission) first as Sheriff and then, dignified and courteous, as Clerk of the Court, serving through the long years without salary, but with the reasonable hope of reversion to an office which he greatly valued and, in the end, unobtrusively adorned.

I recall Sir Walter Scott, great poet, great master of romantic imagination, dining with the douce lawyers ; sharing with sly enjoyment those conceptions of legal pleasantry which do not always appeal to laymen ; and not shrinking from the warm and generous potations which have fre-quently confounded the weaker heads of legal guests. I recall, too, the bitter and, as it seemed, the deep-seated rupture of his first romance in vivid youth. Alas ! my Lord and Ladies, most of us are old enough to know that romantic wounds are, in the main, curable, and most of them —a saying harsh to youth—within a fugitive period. Therefore the tears which, had we not known what was to be—the exquisite happiness of his actual marriage—we might have expended on his failure to indulge the first passion of vehement youth, may be arrested, superfluous and unshed.

When I think of that period in his career, I like also to re-create the man in the eye of my mind as success gradually enabled him to become a laird and a proprietor of land. Such an advancement was evidently always in his mind. He could never resist buying a farm. He must always be adding to his acres. And I recall his incredible labours, rendered tolerable, I suspect, by this land hunger. He rose, as you know, to begin his writing at five o'clock in the morning. He wrote standing always, after he became Laird of Abbotsford, because " he had enough sitting in the discharge of his duties." He wrote—tirelessly, infinitely, beautifully—until failing health made it physically impossible for him to write more. Every word of these unforgettable novels was in his own delicate and exquisite handwriting. I had an opportunity of examining, thirty years ago, many of the manuscripts which the late Mr. Ruskin treasured in that library which looked upon the delightful waters of Coniston.

It is hard indeed in these days, when writers

of the greatest eminence summon a stenographer, to be followed in the background by a typist, to realise the actual physical labour which was necessary in order that this sincere and untiring craftsman might produce the great work of years which we know as the Waverley novels. I ask attention to the courage and resource of the man. When he was already well advanced in the fifties, by no fault, as you know, of his own, except that a very much occupied man was generously—almost disdainfully—careless of his own interests, he had the misfortune to become involved through the negligence (I use to-night no harsher term) of the Ballantynes and Constables in pecuniary embarrassments which to any other living man than Scott would have seemed to be insoluble and even desperate. When the accounts were fully adjusted, it became evident that the irregularities of those whom he had trusted, assisted by his own recklessness, had involved him in liabilities amounting to more than £100,000. In a staggering and poignant moment he displayed a reserve of courage, and a moral resilience, which were not exceeded in physical dourness by any of his soldier-ancestors.

He devoted himself forthwith to the task of extinguishing that debt ; and I need only remind you that at the time when he sustained this most grave—as it must have seemed, this irretrievable —blow he was already conscious of a sharpness of disease sometimes driving him from the dinner table with screams of pain which even his strong courage could not conquer. Nor was that weakness any new thing. Scott's earliest recollections were of lying on the floor, wrapped in the skin of a newly killed sheep and being enticed by his grandfather to crawl painfully towards him. His deformity did not prevent the enjoyment of fair general health in youth and middle age. He possessed, indeed, considerable muscular power in boyhood and early manhood, but as early as 1817 he was a martyr to violent internal pains, and when *Ivanhoe* appeared, his suffering was so constantly acute that his amanuensis, frightened by his moans, would beg him to stop dictating, only to be told, "See that the doors are fast; I would fain keep all the cry, as well as the wool, to ourselves. As to giving up the work, that can only be when I am in woollen."

Such was the man, such the feebleness of his health, while he spent himself inexorably upon the last task of all. In those years, by a prodigy of exertion never exceeded even by the incredibly industrious novelists of France, Hugo, Balzac,

Dumas, and Zola, he repaid, before he died, the creditors (only in the moral field *his* creditors) £62,000 of the total obligation ; and when his copyrights were finally disposed of, when the last contribution was made by the second greatest biographer whom these islands have ever produced, his devoted son-in-law, Lockhart, the uttermost penny of an indebtedness, in those days immense, was discharged.

My Lords, ladies and gentlemen, in this matter neither Scott nor his publishers have escaped censure. The issue indeed was not entirely one-sided. Scott may have reposed unwise, because excessive, trust in the men who linked him with the great reading public ; his rashness in assuming personal responsibility for heavy bills due by his firm was of a piece with the impetuosity of his character ; Lockhart may have over-stated Scott's ignorance of the ramifications of business, and must (I think) have turned a half-closed eye to the large drafts his father-in-law drew for building and other current expenses. The systematic method of bill-discounting was well open to reproach. Scott's own words cannot be overlooked : " I owe it to Ballantyne to say that his difficulties, as well as his advantages, are owing to me." All this, and perhaps more, can be, and has been, quite justly alleged ; the shield without a shadow belongs only to the realms of fancy. But even those who attribute a full—and probably an undue—measure of blame to Scott for many things which conduced to the crash of 1825, agree that his subsequent handling of his affairs was heroic. Bankruptcy, with its coat of financial whitewash, suggested itself—and was suggested to him—as an easy way of dealing with his creditors, who on the whole showed leniency and courtesy ; bankruptcy would have done nothing to dull Scott's literary fame, and little to disturb his normal life. But the ruined old man waved it away. " I will be their vassal for life, and dig in the mine of my imagination, to find diamonds to make good my engagements and not to enrich myself."

Apart from the feeling evidently prevalent that the failure of a great national hero to satisfy his obligations would have been treason to his whole conception of life, it is pleasant, and not amiss, to note at this crisis the attitude of those who touched Scott's life most nearly. His daughter's music-master asked to contribute all his savings towards the deficit ; Sir William Forbes, familiar friend and successful rival in his first love-affair, settled a demand of £2,000 which might have

involved arrest, and kept the transaction secret ;
the old farmer, Laidlaw, who was perforce ejected
by the trustees from his holding, came every week
to walk and talk with his patron ; the coach-
man became ploughman-in-ordinary ; the butler
halved his wages and doubled his work ; and there
was not a former dependent who did not exhibit
the same tokens of loyal affection.

My Lords, ladies and gentlemen, even in these
days when writers reap large rewards, one finds it
difficult to realise that Walter Scott amassed, by
his exertions, a bondsman in the service of those
to whom he was debtor, over £40,000 between
January 1826 and January 1828. His almost
incredible labours undoubtedly shortened—if they
did not end—his life. In 1829 his symptoms
seriously alarmed his friends ; a year later came
a swift stroke of paralysis. Still he clung grimly,
almost desperately, to pen, ink, and paper. The
time, he saw, was short. There was still much
ground to be regained. He laboured on, and his
labours fell in quality little below their former
level. Then, with the second numbing stroke,
a veil began slowly to drop across the tired
memory ; he became possessed—did Providence
ever permit a happier delusion ?—of the idea that
his debts were paid ; that his commercial honour

was vindicated ; and that he was free to go and do as he pleased. The physicians recommended a sea-voyage ; he had hitherto been deaf to all entreaties that he would rest the weak body and relax the overstrained mind. Now foreign scenes and climates beckoned alluringly to him ; the Government placed a vessel at his disposal, and for more than a year there was pure enjoyment in a cruise on the Mediterranean waters, and in visiting places of absorbing interest. But when the end was drawing near, Scotland and the " misty sheilings " irresistibly claimed him, and with imperious will-power he insisted on being carried across Europe to die where he lived, and was loved, at Abbotsford.

He was a great Scot, a great gentleman, a great Briton ; and there would be justification in his example to the youth of Scotland and England, had he never written a word which the reasoned judgment of posterity pronounced to be worthy of survival, for the existence of your club and for the admiration which year by year you show to the memory of this illustrious man.

But there were other sides of him which are intimately in the minds of all of you to-night. I ask leave to say of him a few words first in the capacity of poet ; and then to make some obser-

vations upon that astonishing series of novels
which I am persuaded will endure as long as the
English language is spoken or written.

I have often read of the contemporary impression which was made by the appearance of *The Lay
of the Last Minstrel*. It created a sensation on both
sides of the Border as great as that produced by
the fundamentally different work, upon the publication of which it was said that in one night
Byron woke up and found himself famous. Many
explanations might be made, if the right attitude
of mind is indeed to require an explanation, of the
swift and sudden success of Scott's work. Let
me attempt one or two. In the first place, there
was a treasure-house of material for him who had
the observation to discern, and the genius to
exploit it, lying hid in the romantic periods of
Scottish history, which up to that time had almost
entirely escaped the industry or the attention of
your Scottish poets. Indeed, it is not one of the
smallest services which he rendered to literature,
and to the history and national traditions of
Scotland, that he most clearly saw that not only
was there here a vast and inexhaustibly rich
subject-matter, but that it was one which lent
itself in particular degree to the special gifts which
he alone possessed.

Contemporary literature was not rich in poets to whose genius it could reasonably be hoped that such a romantic topic would make a promising appeal. The world had passed far beyond the smooth, barbed, artificial alexandrines of the period of Pope ; Cowper, with all his finesse and tact, with all his homely intimacy of sympathy and perception, lived in another age ; Coleridge had neither found his audience nor attained the full stature of his genius ; and suddenly there arose in this small country of yours, with a population relatively insignificant, one of the consummate ballad-makers of the world.

Higher praise cannot very easily be given to a poet. It may be a more sonorous eulogy to aver that such a one is a master of poignant tragedy ; of another that his art has conquered the very spirit of exquisite lyric ; but to claim for a poet, who comes himself of a martial race, that he has reproduced in stirring poesy the soul of a fighting people ; has re-created the traditions and per-sonalities of an age, vanished indeed, but to be born and reborn in the passage of the centuries— this is a tribute to Scott which, had he never set pen to prose, would still leave him high among the Immortals of song.

I have often thought, though the relatively

abrupt metre which Scott adopted suffers, as an instrument of heroic exposition, in comparison with the majestic, flexible, and musical hexameters of Homer, that he belongs none the less to the men who were labourers in that school of Greek ballad-art which, if the theories of modern scholars be well founded, produced, as a result of composite effort, those matchless efforts of genius which many of us still choose to associate with a single name.

I cannot doubt that Walter Scott was of the spirit and company of those gay and vivid troubadours who journeyed through the ballad-loving cities of Greece, singing their sweet songs beneath its violet skies. William of Deloraine, Roderick Dhu, the Last Minstrel, the Duchess of Buccleuch— name after name springs to mind when one thinks of the remarkable technique, marred here and there perhaps by an element of crudity, but redeemed by an artistry which is only realised after repeated and painstaking analysis.

I am sure that there has been no poet since Scott wrote who has taught so attractively to adventurous youth the story and the gallantry of the past ; who has taught it more to the profit of the present ; more to the hope of the future. I am sufficiently a believer in the teaching of

Scott to be sure that neither is this world now, nor hereafter will it be, an easy world to live in. I have never been able to persuade myself that the arms of the strong will not again and again be required by Britain in the years that lie in front of us. Let us by all means devote every influence of which we are masters to avoid war; but do not let us be so blind to the teachings of history as to believe that great possessions will be permitted in the future of the world to soft peoples. They never have been; they never will be. I incurred some censure in a speech which I made at Glasgow a year ago, and which was only liable to censure (if at all) because it contained so many platitudes. It was an address founded upon the philosophy and teaching of Sir Walter Scott.

I for one believe, recalling the unforgettable achievements of so many Scottish soldiers in the crucible of that war through which we have so lately passed; recalling the glorious part they played, to take one example among many, in that unhappy battle of Loos in which the largest Scottish army marched which has ever assembled under one banner; that we must realise how much the soldierly spirit of a race naturally martial has been nourished by Walter Scott. Scotland, by her supreme efforts, surpassed her own exalted traditions. She stood foursquare, the equal comrade of England, of Canada, of Australia.

I pass in natural order to the subject of Scott's novels. No more interesting literary chapter has ever been written than that concerned with the anonymity which he preserved over so long a period of years. In one of the introductions—I think it is the introduction to *Waverley* (I speak from memory)—he discussed the ethics of anonymous production, and the honourable obligation of an author, who, deliberately choosing to withhold his name, is asked point-blank whether or not he is in fact the author of his book. Scott argues, in the first place, that a man is entitled to protect his own secret in such a case ; and, in the second, that, if this be admitted, he must be entitled to meet impertinence by reticence. But it must be observed that the word " reticence " is somewhat inadequate alike to the necessities of the case and to the ambit of the argument, because if a man asks, "Are you the author of *Waverley* ? and you reply, " I decline to make any statement on the matter," the purpose of the questioner will be fully achieved. I cannot myself doubt that the teaching of Sir Walter Scott (and I infer also, his practice) was to preserve a secret which he conceived to be his own by any bluntness of affirmation or negation which he found necessary for his purpose.

The limits indeed of permissible mendacity, if there be such, have long been the subject of interesting ethical debate. One remembers the old assumption that in no circumstances was a positive falsehood permitted to a man of honour. But a test has been applied. Supposing you are standing at a point at which five different roads diverge. A terror-stricken wretch runs past and takes one of these roads. Seven minutes later six armed villains follow in hot pursuit and ask you which road he has taken. What is your answer to be ? You may, of course, answer that you did not see him. That would not be true. You may refuse to answer at all, but I have already supposed that the villains were armed, and, therefore, on the whole, one would perhaps think it proper to answer. I believe—indeed I hope—that you would lie.

I do not pursue these topics further, full of interest as they are ; but I make the observation how singular it was that, over this long period of years, so few people really knew that Scott had written these romances. Almost exactly a hundred years ago, and in this ancient city, the authoritative announcement was first made that Scott was the author of the Waverley novels.

I cannot, in any time available to me, even attempt to measure the quality of his stories, still less to estimate their permanent place in literature. To me it seems certain that they must occupy one of the highest places, if only because their begetter was almost the pioneer of adventurous romance. No one had ever adjusted to the form of the novel, romantic literature in the sense in which he conceived and expressed it. The world of letters had wept over the long-drawn-out and maudlin sentimentality of Richardson ; had reviewed the long-postponed seduction of Clarissa ; the robust humour, the high spirit, the humanity of Fielding ; the cynical, ironical, and coarse brilliancy of Sterne. And there were women writers, too, almost of the same period, whose charm and ingenuity still deservedly command the admiration of discriminating readers. It remains nevertheless broadly true that Scott was the pioneer of those romances which commingle, in subtle alchemy, the atmospheres of adventure and love ; and it remains equally true that, ever since he wrote his novels, the reading taste of the world has more and more inclined towards the imaginative and adventurous among story-tellers. Scott was the true father of Stevenson. What a father ! What a son !

Consider how vast was the canvas upon which

he painted, how versatile and fecund the brush,
how vivid the pigment. He wrote, indeed, upon
the scale and with the range of the greatest
masters of French literature. It is certain that the
exuberant genius of Dumas owed much to the
full-blooded yet literary pages of Scott; and I
never watch the Three Musketeers galloping from
Boulogne without recalling that they paid a debt
to the dreams of adventure so brilliantly flung
into words by him who was Dumas's master.
Did Dumas, I wonder, know how much Scott
owed in rhythm (or thought he owed) to his
gallops on Musselburgh sands?

And now, I ask you only to consider the number
of Scott's stories; to consider the variety of his
plots; to consider, if you assembled in one room
the immense number of characters created by him,
possessing in almost every case a distinct and
enduring individuality, how wise, how witty,
how brave, how beautiful the company! What
would one give to meet them as an inconspicuous
guest?

Nor, as I have indicated, would it be right to
dismiss him from the British point of view with
the light and almost disparaging observation
that, after all, he was particularly if not entirely
a Scottish author, a Scottish hero. Sometimes

it is put almost as if some barbarity or obsolescence of diction made it impossible that he should be generally appreciated or even generally understood in England. Wider nonsense was never talked. We are not so simple as is sometimes supposed. I have little knowledge of the Scottish dialect—I had none until, for my sins, I was led to acquire some acquaintance with the Scottish feudal law—but I am bound to make it plain that I never felt difficulty in understanding any of Scott's allusiveness, or indeed any of his language. I make a still further claim. I say that, if he had never written one Scottish romance, he would yet be entitled to live for ever in the pages of an English anthology, prosaic or poetic. For he showed himself to be as capable of understanding the soul of St. George, the underlying essence of premediæval England, as of harping melodiously and forcefully on the strings of your own storied clannish life. What is *Ivanhoe* but the very spirit of St. George and England? Robin Hood is painted with a touch as masterly and as faithful to English tradition as *Rob Roy* is to your conception of the character of that bold Scottish adventurer.

Walter Scott was in fact almost as eloquent a witness to the genius and patriotism of England

as to the genius and patriotism of Scotland. I
recall here that so lavish, so prodigal, was he of
stray lines of poetry that much of his best may have
perished (for the authorship of it) for ever. He
often treated his poetry like his money affairs.
He has carelessly prefaced many of the chapters
of his romances by verses which another would
have collected with care, and published with
complacency. This brings me to one of the
strangest paradoxes in literary history :

> " Sound, sound the clarion, fill the fife !
> To all the sensual world proclaim,
> One crowded hour of glorious life
> Is worth an age without a name."

For sixty years it was not only supposed that this
verse was written by Walter Scott, but it was
conceived that it was the very embodiment, in
its highest and most eloquent expression, of his
gay and daring philosophy of life. And quite
recently it became known that these lines, which
he himself described as anonymous, had been
published in a comparatively unknown periodical
in the course of a poem which contained not
another distinguished line, and which was not
otherwise known to the literature either of Scotland or England. Some faithful Scot lately wrote
to a literary paper in London that Sir Walter

Scott, with his accustomed generosity, may have been asked to read over an anonymous poem by an unknown contemporary, and may have contributed the one jewel it contained. I should like to believe that this was true. A lawyer, alas! cannot so believe.

And so, by way of ending, I add an alien, if affectionate, tribute to the majestic edifice of that fame which has spread over all the civilised world. As I look back on that long, unselfish, noble, toilful, and patriotic life, I take pleasure in borrowing the words of a young English poet, written of a friend who lost his life in a water-sodden trench :

" Oh strong, Oh brave, Oh true! Farewell."

IV

LAW AND THE PUBLIC

VERY surprising statements have been published as to the legal cost incurred in certain
recent litigation. It has, for instance, been
alleged that the total expenditure incurred by
both sides amounted to no less a sum than
£60,000. I do not for a moment believe this statement; but that the cost of the case was very
great cannot be doubted. The notoriety which
this particular matter procured has revived a
general and familiar discussion as to whether or
not law and lawyers do in fact cost too much.

We may begin by assuming that 90 per cent.
of laymen would answer the question with a short
and sharp affirmative. The existence of such
practical unanimity amongst those who are pay-
masters of lawyers is a very important element
in that falling-off of litigation of which the Bar
to-day so bitterly complains. If the amount at
issue between A and B is £10,000; if the costs
of the unsuccessful litigant may conceivably
amount to an almost equal sum; and if the

result of the case is not absolutely certain, most litigants will prefer to make a reasonable compromise rather than embark upon these perilous financial waters. It would not, therefore, be in the interests of the legal profession itself should the notion gain ground that the law is so expensive that it no longer pays to contest even a reasonable case. Yet in fairness certain considerations should be borne in mind, which do in part explain the very considerable increase in the cost of legal proceedings which has been observable in the last ten years.

In the first place, lawyers, like everyone else, have to pay more for their food, for rent, for clothes, and for taxes. It cannot be supposed reasonable that they should meet all these embarrassing increases, and yet themselves charge only the same fees as satisfied them before the war. The total cost of renting an office must, I suppose, have increased by about 30 per cent. since the war. It must, in the second place, be borne in mind that the contrast is hardly fair between the comparative brevity of the old cases and the extraordinary length of many modern proceedings. For, in the first place, in the old days there were no telegrams or cablegrams; even letters were few, for it took so long to deliver them.

Hence the bundle of correspondence in the old days which had to be read to the Court was usually extremely meagre. To-day, in a heavy commercial case, it may occupy six or seven hundred pages of a bulky correspondence bundle, which must be examined in court.

The increasing length of criminal proceedings is, in my judgment, to be explained in two ways. To begin, the existence of the Court of Criminal Appeal has, in the most salutary manner, increased the carefulness of Judges sitting in Courts of First Instance. I have formed the clear conclusion that prosecutions are more deliberately and more thoroughly conducted now than they were before the right of appeal in criminal cases was established. This is all to the good, for no time can be really excessive which even in remote contingency may afford a person accused of crime a better opportunity of demonstrating his innocence.

Another very important advance in this connection must be borne in mind. Not many years ago an extremely important and even a revolutionary change was made in the law of evidence in criminal cases. It was after long controversy enacted that a person accused of crime should be an available, though not a compellable, witness in his own behalf. The law which made this change was very solicitous in the interest of the prisoner ; for it provided that, if he did not present himself in the witness-box, opposing counsel should not be permitted to comment upon his omission ; though the Judge in his discretion might do so. Yet it has in practice so worked out that all juries realise that a prisoner can, if he chooses and has confidence in his powers to resist the cross-examination, tender himself as a witness on his own behalf. Juries, therefore, draw their own inferences from the refusal of the prisoner to go into the box. And so in practice it happens that counsel for the defence will hardly ever take the responsibility of advising a prisoner not to give evidence.

Consider the change which that has made in the duration of criminal trials. In cases like those of Crippen or Mahon or Thorne, two or three days can easily be consumed in the examination and cross-examination of the prisoner ; and so a matter which in the old days would have concluded in one day may easily last four or five. And we must not make the mistake of supposing that long-drawn-out litigation is the perverse innovation of our own times. In correction of a view so rash, and making some allowance for the amateur constitution of the tribunal, we may recall the years that were consumed over the trial of Warren Hastings ; and in modern times the immense period which was occupied from first to last in the Tichborne case.

It must, nevertheless, be plainly admitted by any candid lawyer that there is much judicial time wasted on circuit. I myself, when Lord Chancellor, most strongly urged upon the Coalition Government the necessity of reform in this matter. It is, no doubt, very desirable that in every important centre of population the dignity and majesty of the law should be made apparent. But in such matters we must strike a balance in relation to modern conditions. With full knowledge of the facts, I affirm that the present arrangements of the circuit business involve the most flagrant waste of judicial time. It is, on the face of it, ludicrous to suppose that we have stereotyped for all time those centres of population which are entitled to hold Assizes. It would have been as reasonable to admit stereotyped pocket boroughs. Populations have moved. The importance of one place has declined ; of another has grown. It is, in fact, no exaggeration to say that in the smaller circuit towns 50 per cent. of the time of our Judges is uselessly squandered. The question will probably be asked : Why has such a system not been altered ? The answer is perfectly plain. It defeated me in the year 1919. It is because local political influence is violently exerted to prevent reform ; and there is no available political influence upon the other side. The task of a Lord Chancellor is very hard when he has all the politicians against him, the majority of the lawyers, and only a minority tepidly with him.

A word or two may be added upon the practical question whether a client having a case in which he believes, need spend, in order to give that case a chance, the very large sums which are undoubtedly paid to-day. In my opinion he need not. The ordinary client seems to me to make the mistake that he does not take advantage of the very great competition that exists both among solicitors and barristers. He may, of course, if he chooses, go to an extremely fashionable and successful firm of solicitors. In this case he pays, and rightly pays, for the reputation of the firm ; for the rent of its offices, and for the salaries that are paid to many experienced clerks. But there are countless firms of solicitors, quite honest and quite efficient, who are neither so fashionable as to command very high fees nor so

busily occupied as to refuse work for which a
reasonable remuneration is offered. Perhaps in
such a case the partner will attend to the matter
instead of the managing clerk. Perhaps, also,
in such a case the client will not be a loser by the
substitution. The same remark is at least
equally true of the Bar. There always exist two
or three fashionable leaders at the Bar who
command very surprising fees, and do not always
find it convenient even to make an appearance in
court in order to earn them. Few members of
the Bar would go to such men if they became
involved in litigation themselves. For the plain
truth is that there are always at least twenty or
thirty members of the Bar who could act as advocates in any case—from *Nisi Prius* to the House
of Lords—with the most complete efficiency, and
whose business engagements enable them to give
sustained and continuous attention to the cases
in which they are employed.

Personally, if I became involved in litigation,
the consequences of which were grave to me, I
would infinitely rather be represented by A, a
competent and industrious lawyer, who I knew
would not leave the court from the moment my
case began until the moment it ended, than by
B, who would, at ten times the fee, saunter into

court to cross-examine a witness whose examination-in-chief he had not heard, or to reply to a speech which had unfortunately been delivered in his absence. I reach, therefore, the conclusion that in cases where colossal sums are spent upon litigation, the fault is as often as not chargeable upon the clients themselves. You can spend as much as you choose upon surgeons, counsel, dentists, and tailors, but it by no means follows that he who pays most is best served.

.   .   .   .   .   .

It is no part of my object to write a treatise of the law and practice relating to costs, nor to sketch the history of the present system. In calling attention now to some of its anomalies, it does not follow that I affirm that there are no others or that I advocate any particular amendment or change. It is the general aspect of the question that is the more important—the bearing of professional charges upon the relations between the lawyers and the public.

There are now many professions or quasi-professions which make demands on the national income, and the lawyer's share is but one factor in a problem of great interest. The profession exists solely because it is necessary for the public welfare and is entitled to remuneration in pro-

portion to its services. The general gibe is that
lawyers are grasping and make too much money.
It is on the lips of those who in some cases earn
large incomes but could not point to any service
of the slightest possible value to the community,
and in all probability if it were of any use to
formulate comparisons the familiar taunt would
be found to be an ancient fiction. What the
public does feel is a very real grievance : it is
charged a high rate for mechanical service. It
does not realise that it is frequently not charged
at all for the real service rendered.

As is so often the case in England, the reason
is that the system has been developed by slow
degrees in the course of centuries. The status
of solicitors changed during the course of the
nineteenth century and the change has resulted
in an immense improvement in their work and
social standing. How far and to what extent
this has been accomplished at the expense of the
Bar, and whether thereby the legal profession has
lost the spheres appropriated by accountants,
estate agents, election agents, and the like,
are inquiries which deserve serious detailed
attention ; but the fact of the change must
be noted because the principles underlying the
system of remuneration were settled when a

solicitor, with exceptions which are not material for this discussion, was in fact little more than a person skilled in the details and clerical work of lawsuits. Principles thus settled in conditions which have radically changed are apt to cease to be fair and just. They may give too much or too little in particular cases. It can rarely happen that they ever give the right amount. The fundamental conception underlying the various rules applicable to costs is that they are the reward of services mainly of a clerical nature. That conception is no longer wholly true. Nevertheless, it has elements of abiding truth, since the conduct of litigation and the ordinary affairs of clients does involve the giving, if only vicariously, of many services which are purely clerical.

There is, however, a new and different conception that must be considered. The solicitor is nowadays a skilled adviser. Many of the leaders of the profession are so occupied with clients that they hardly do anything else. The work of the office is necessarily delegated to others, but it is that delegated work which is the main source of inspiration to the framers of scales of costs. Everyone is familiar with the jest that a solicitor once put in his bill an item " To lying awake thinking of your case." It owes its point to the fact

that time spent in writing, in reading, and other
clerical operations finds its way into the bill;
but time spent in thought does not. Indeed, it
may actually diminish the bill. A familiar example is the drafting of a brief. One man may
spend much time and thought in considering the
form and arrangement of the observations, so
that counsel may " get up " the case quickly and
without unnecessary reading. The result is a
clear, concise brief directed to the real issues.
Another man may pour forth a long and confused
commentary on the issues and the evidence,
taking them up as they occur to him, producing
a verbose, confused, and confusing document
of little value, which may be even worse than
useless. The latter is of much more value to the
solicitor's banking account than the former.
The former is of infinitely more use to the client,
who pays less for it. That is an example, which
could be improved upon by any costs clerk.
There are many ways of increasing a bill of costs,
but it would be impossible to allege with truth
that the additional items relate to the services
which are of real value. Indeed, it would be
easy for such a clerk to multiply instances in
which his employer's care and skill have been
so successfully used as to spoil the bill altogether.

Another instance, of a different character, is the singular fact that, merely because of the clerical charges for copying, a solicitor is better remunerated for a County Court case if he briefs counsel than if he does the case himself. It is not merely a question of counsel's fee; the solicitor's fee for doing less of the work himself and being able if need be to delegate all that work to an unqualified assistant is actually greater. This anomaly, by reason of the greater frequency of the occasions on which it occurs, mulcts clients in favour of their solicitors to a far greater extent than does the " two-thirds rule " which applies as a rule when more than one barrister is briefed.

The present system leads to the anomaly that a solicitor's remuneration does not necessarily correspond with the real services that he renders and may have little relation to it. If, therefore, on balance he is paid sufficient, he must be over-paid for some services while being underpaid for others. Some such result cannot be avoided altogether, for general rules must lead to par-ticular anomalies, but it is a matter for solicitors to consider whether their reward is as justly proportioned to the nature of the services as is desirable. Too great an anomaly will inevitably result, in effect, in one client contributing towards another's bill. The task must, however, be undertaken by solicitors themselves. They alone have the necessary material and experience to prepare the " brief " for any revision. I shall point out later that fusion, if ever it came about, would necessitate a thorough overhaul of the system of charging fees. Adherents of that proposal might well do some spade-work to further their aims by considering this question by comparison with counsel's fees, and thereby perhaps some advance may be made in modernising the solicitor's part of the fees question.

Another anomaly is the fact that the same services may be rewarded by different sums, according, not to their necessity or importance, but to the Court in which proceedings may be taken. The scales in the various Courts are different. In Police Courts it may almost be said that there is no scale, and the rough-and-ready adjudication by justices of the prosecution's costs is often more truly proportioned to the work than the most elaborate bill by items according to scale. Where litigation is at all lengthy, some scale must be used, but it is perhaps difficult wholly to justify the fact that work in the various Courts is not necessarily charged according to a uniform scale. There is no doubt a general correspondence between the scales adopted by various Courts, but solicitors might well consider whether in every Court and in all proceedings the same uniform method of fixing their charges should not prevail, due care being taken that exceptional cases may receive exceptional treatment.

It will never be possible to eliminate the distinction between " solicitor and client " and " party and party costs." A successful litigant should receive an indemnity for the costs reasonably necessary to bring about the result, but the defeated party is not delivered to him bound hand and foot to pay for services, rendered no doubt to the successful party, which are in the nature of luxuries. The victor's excessive caution or extravagance is no reason for calling upon the defeated one to pay for the costs thereby incurred ; but it is also no reason why they should be paid for by nobody. Every costs clerk, however, is furnished with examples where work which no prudent solicitor would refrain from doing will not be allowed for on taxation. The taxing masters have a difficult and exacting task, which they discharge with great care, but they are not entitled either to legislate or to innovate.

The system of taxation, with the preliminary
work of preparing bills, is involved and complicated. Few understand the work and no
client can possibly be expected to have more than
the vaguest idea of what is being done. Yet it
is by such means that the amount of his liability
is ascertained. It is a matter for consideration
whether the taxing staff is adequate for really
speedy taxation—a matter of grave importance
when the party liable is in financial difficulties.
It has happened that a solicitor has had to watch
the person liable to pay costs taking care to
render that the order shall be useless and having
the opportunity to do so given him by the
interval that elapses before the taxation can be
completed.

The greatest defect of the present system is its
uncertainty in connection with litigation. To
some extent uncertainty is unavoidable, but it
is a matter of grave concern that no prudent man
can count the cost of contemplated litigation with
any reasonable degree of accuracy. In convey-
ancing practically in every case the exact figure
can be given ; in Police-Court proceedings a sum
can, as a rule, be named to cover the whole cost,
and this is generally true of all criminal trials.
In civil proceedings, even in the County Court

1—8

where the procedure is simpler, an accurate estimate is practically impossible. Uncertainty breeds reluctance to proceed and a desire to adopt other means, if such exist, to accomplish the result, especially in view of the fact that it is quite possible for a plaintiff to win his case and to recover both the sum claimed and the amount of the taxed costs and yet be out of pocket at the end, worse off than if he had waived the claim.

The great desiderata of any system of payment for services are reasonableness and certainty. Charges are not reasonable unless they bear a just proportion to the nature of the services rendered. Unless these requirements are satisfied, dissatisfaction is inevitable and will be felt on both sides.

It is impossible in the course of a short survey to deal adequately with any individual question, still less to touch upon all. I have, therefore, omitted many matters which have a great interest both to the public and to the profession. It is only right, however, to mention that solicitors, both in connection with the Law Courts and in many other ways, often give their services gratuitously or for nominal fees out of public spirit and a sense of charity, for which they do not often receive the thanks that are justly due to them.

But this is not strictly relevant to the problems which arise when their fees for ordinary work are under discussion.

Revision need not necessarily mean an increase of fees. Times are hard and many are competing for the national income. Solicitors as a body are anxious only that their remuneration shall be fair and just, and have no desire to make comparisons, which, if made, would prove that the legal profession has a lot to learn in the gentle art of making a meal out of the public and might indeed for ever remove the popular reproach. Revision, if it be needed and if it be effected, must be limited to the one aim of securing that payment shall be reasonable and bear a true proportion to the services rendered. The fact that the master's brain-work is paid by the labour of the clerk's pen renders the existing principle of costs inadequate. It does not necessarily follow that the total of the bill ought to be greater.

.   .   .   .   .   .

The present division of the legal profession into barristers and solicitors is of comparatively recent origin. Without recalling remote antiquity, when attorneys, notaries, proctors, scriveners, and solicitors all did work which in one form or another is now classed as solicitors' work, it is sufficient to say that this branch of the profession was only formed by amalgamation in Victorian days, and it may even be suggested that Parliamentary agents do solicitors' work within the sphere without necessarily being solicitors.

The Bar, too, has acquired its modern development in times equally recent. It is not long since the last Sergeant-at-Law died, and only a short time separated his death from those of the last Advocate, the last Conveyancer, and the last Special Pleader practising under the Bar. There was a time when no barrister had audience in the Court of Common Pleas, in the Court of Admiralty, or in any Ecclesiastical Court.

While these changes were being made, the creation of County Courts and the reorganisation of the Courts of Justices of the Peace under the Acts of 1846 and 1848 and subsequent statutes introduced a new kind of solicitor, the advocate in County Courts and Police-Courts, and for many years the public has been aware that in those Courts barristers and solicitors co-exist as advocates, neither branch having any peculiar privileges in those Courts as against one another.

As at present organised, barristers form a branch of the legal profession having, with exceptions not material for this purpose, exclusive right of audience in the superior Courts of Record and some other Courts, and concurrent rights with solicitors in most of the lower Courts ; and also fulfilling the duties of consultants, a rôle which is logically distinct from the other.

The suggestion of fusion is frequently made in the form that the exclusive right of audience shall be abolished, so that all lawyers shall have the right to appear as advocates in all Courts. The matter is not so simple, as indeed the great majority of those who have taken part in the discussions have realised. When the exclusive right of audience in the Court of Common Pleas was abolished, it soon became apparent that there was no room for three classes of advocates— the silk, the sergeant, and the stuffgownsman— and the ancient institution of Sergeants-at-Law recognised this fact by abolishing itself. So, too, if the exclusive right of audience ceases to be one of the privileges of the Bar, it may well be that the reason for separation of the two branches may be found to have vanished, and the legal profession, like the sister profession of medicine, may have to evolve its consultants from among those whose qualification in law is the same.

The proposal comes down to this : that every

practising lawyer, be he solicitor or counsel, shall have the same rights, so that a man called at one of the Inns of Court may do all that a solicitor now does, and that everyone who is placed on the rolls shall be entitled to do all that a barrister now does.

For this country the innovation would indeed be startling. The existing organisation of the profession is one almost peculiar to England, and is to a large extent the outcome of conditions which have their origin in the past and their justification in the habits of the present. It is impossible to forecast the consequences. Some guidance may be obtained from the experience of other countries with institutions and procedure similar to our own, but without this division. Some support for prophecy may no doubt be gained from a consideration of other professions which are differently organised; but when all the factors are taken into account, any estimate of the influence on the future of the profession cannot be more than an instructed guess.

The main consideration must be the public welfare. The legal profession can only justify its existence by its service to the public. Unless such a change will be a benefit to the country generally, it has no *raison d'être*.

By the rules of professional etiquette, which could be altered by the common assent of the Bar, the public has, speaking broadly, no direct access to a barrister. In the work of advising and of advocacy this fact enables him to view the problems from a detached and impartial standpoint which is not always easy for a solicitor, who is necessarily brought into close touch with his client ; indeed in the case of large companies and public authorities the solicitor may be an employee of the client. Whether a change would destroy this advantage is a matter upon which opinions may differ. It is a vital consideration when the public interest is considered.

Experience in the United States and the Dominions tends to confirm the impression that an amalgamation of the two branches would not destroy the consultant or the specialist. His position would be vastly different, though how this change could be made manifest cannot be foreseen. In the United States one sees lawyers and the new tax lawyers, to whom clients and even the other lawyers go when they feel the need for special skill and guidance. But the client or his lawyer may not realise that the situation does demand such special handling. The lawyer does not always realise his limitations.

As matters now stand with us, litigation at all events almost necessarily involves a case being placed in the hands of counsel by a solicitor, who is concerned to instruct the right man and is in a position to find out who that man is. In non-litigious matters, everyone is familiar with the problems which often arise from the fact that persons of ordinary competence have handled matters which called for expert treatment.

One may assume with confidence that the advocate or trial lawyer will always flourish. He is in the public mind the barrister *par excellence* ; the tendency is to exalt advocacy above all else, and to regard a man who is brilliant in handling questions of fact as suitable for all litigation. There is not much danger that commercial and business men would ever go far wrong in their estimate of a lawyer's ability, but there are many who only occasionally have need to call upon a lawyer for help, and their views can at present be modified by candid advice from their solicitor. It may be that the removal of this safeguard will not be for the real advantage of the client, and there may be the added danger that through over-confidence or a desire not to forfeit the good opinion of a client a lawyer would be tempted or even feel compelled to appear in cases for which he was not fitted.

I do not wish to dwell on another aspect, which is merely temporary. Clients have a tendency to go straight to the fountain-head. A reorganisation of the Bar into partnerships, with tried leaders as the senior partner, might conceivably attract far more clients away from solicitors than solicitors would gain by being able to conduct cases in the Courts. This is, however, merely a situation which could only arise at a particular stage and concerns only competition between the two branches at that stage.

There is, however, one temporary aspect which would create a difficulty calling for sympathetic handling. A barrister's clerk has very special functions relating to the intercourse between the two branches and, apart from this, he renders only mere clerical assistance to his employer. By his training it is unlikely that a barrister's clerk of any standing in his calling would be able to master the important subordinate working of a managing clerk, whose duties are entirely different from his ; and fusion would mean the inevitable disappearance of a body of worthy men and great and unavoidable hardship to many of them.

Another consequence of great importance both to lawyers and their clients would be the revision of the whole system of charging costs. Solicitors and counsel are at present remunerated by methods which are so dissimilar that they cannot be simply combined or amalgamated. It is not the case that the client would be paying one set of lawyers instead of two as at present ; it is indeed doubtful whether amalgamation would in the long run save expense. Lawyers in the United States seem to earn more, both individually and as a class, than their brethren do here. It may well be that such a change would enable the future lawyer to quote an inclusive fee for an action. It is one of the defects of the present system that no solicitor, however experienced, can advise his clients except with vague approximation what the commencing of litigation will mean in costs, even when only the client's own costs are in question.

It is possible that fusion would tend to lower the general legal knowledge of lawyers. It might be that the ablest lawyers would thereafter all be so absorbed in the task of advising clients that it would be impossible for them to attain any deep knowledge of law. It is possible that the best lawyers would be found dealing with

matters arising in the borderland which lies between law and business, leaving the law to young
and subordinate lawyers. The rewards of the
advocate and of the business lawyer might
take all the real intellect of the profession and
thereby do the public no good.

At present, the topic is one of interest rather
than practical politics. But it may become a
burning question at any time. If the Bar were
faced with a demand for complete equalisation
supported by the whole body of solicitors, they
would find it difficult, if not impossible, to refuse.
I have endeavoured shortly and without develop-
ing them to indicate some of the more salient
features of the problem, rather with a view to
guide discussion than to take sides upon a matter
where there is room for doubt and difference.

To sum up : The problem is one which is
hardly at present within range of practical politics, but may become so at any time. If the
Bar is faced with a demand, supported by an
overwhelming body of opinion from the solicitors,
a refusal would be difficult, and it would be wiser
to yield on terms than run the risk of having the
change imposed from without. In considering
the problem, it must be borne in mind that the
matter is not simple but highly complex, involv-

ing a reconsideration of the position of both branches of the profession and the solution of many difficulties which now are hardly perceived but which will call urgently for immediate attention once a change has been effected. For my part, I would advise advocates of fusion to proceed with care and deliberation and to reflect upon the wisdom of the ancient maxim *Quieta non movere.*

In this, as in all other questions affecting the welfare of the legal profession, the fundamental principle must be the advantage of the public.

V

BREACH OF PROMISE OF MARRIAGE

"TIME we were off, my dear sir; breach of promise trial—Court is generally full in such cases," said Perker on a memorable occasion. The observation has always been as true as it was then. Breach of promise cases are invariably well attended and reported in the newspapers. The public interest is counterbalanced by a body of opinion which would abolish or curtail these actions. It is not difficult to explain this aversion from such cases. Most disappointed lovers shrink from the publicity of an action. All men who have been jilted would be well advised not to run the hazard of an action in which the sympathy of the Judge and jury will certainly not be in favour of a man who makes such a complaint of his woes. At one time there was a feeling that money should not be made out of a death. Life was of inestimable value; the innocent sufferer, therefore, should have no redress and the taker of the precious life should go free from any obligation. The rule has been altered, but there are still traces of its influence.

When, however, the nature of a breach of promise action is considered, it cannot be distinguished in principle from any other action founded upon breach of contract. A promise has been made and broken. Loss has ensued, and that loss is measured by the verdict of a jury. The principles upon which the damages are assessed do not differ from those principles for assessing damages in any other case where exact estimation is impossible. It is said that this is distinguished from all other causes of action upon contract by reason of the jury being able to award exemplary damages. It is no doubt true that the jury do have regard to the conduct of the defendant, so that the more heartless the conduct the greater is the chance of obtaining heavy damages. Nevertheless, the award in such cases can be supported on the same ground as in other cases, viz. that unless the jury can be shown to have gone wrong on a point of principle, their verdict will not be upset.

The remedy, of course, is not a perfect one. Most women of delicacy and refinement shrink from making a claim. No man of normal feeling would attempt to bring such an action unless driven to it by a combination of circumstances which can hardly be imagined ever to have happened. The plaintiff therefore is suspect ; it is assumed that her feelings are not the most sensitive, and, if the defendant's counsel can laugh the matter out of Court, it is often the best defence. A breath of frivolity frequently invades the solemn atmosphere of the Courts, and the spectators and the readers of newspapers enjoy a real comedy at little or no cost to themselves.

It is no doubt difficult for a plaintiff to impress the jury that she is neither heartless nor foolish, but why the termination of a relation which should be hardly less sacred than the marriage tie should be the occasion for mirth at the expense of the unhappy pair is one of the mysteries of human existence. While this state of affairs continues many cruel wrongs will go without redress, because the injured party refuses to run the risk of being a show to a thoughtless crowd seeking amusement at her expense. No such criticism can be levied at the conduct of proceedings for divorce. The shipwreck of marriage is treated, and rightly so, as a serious matter, and an injured spouse, whether man or woman, who comes to the Divorce Court for redress is treated by the public, as well as the Court, as a person who must not be regarded as an involuntary subject for the exercise of humour.

An objection to this form of action is that it may be made a means of blackmail. That is true, and the fact is recognised by the Court insisting upon corroboration. But that such an action may be brought from improper motives is a comment which may be made on practically all causes of action. It is no doubt because the plaintiff is often a person to whom redress is due that the fraudulent plaintiff uses the threat of such proceedings, but no honest person who has suffered wrong should be deprived of a remedy merely because some other person may falsely pretend that such is also the case with her. It is the duty of the Judge and jury to distinguish the plaintiff who ought to succeed from the plaintiff who deserves to lose, and if (as seldom happens) the task is not duly and properly performed, the remedy is not to shut out all litigants, but to strengthen the hands of the tribunal so that the trial may again become the touchstone of truth. It is, of course, no answer to say that a man or woman should not so behave as to be open to blackmail. For such a one the blackmailer never has had terrors, but, though the foolish and imprudent need protection, it should

not be at the expense of those who have suffered
injury at the hands of another.

The objections which strike at the existence of
this action are based on the feeling, which should
not be misunderstood or underestimated, that
the Courts should not be called upon to adjudi-
cate between the parties to such a contract. A
lawsuit between lovers, *lis amantium*, is a contra-
diction in terms, but the world is not a place
for idealists only.   Lovers cease to love, and the
law provides a means for settling disputes.   A
more specious suggestion is that these actions
should be confined to the award of " special
damage," the actual money loss.   This amendment of the law would concentrate too materially
upon the merely monetary aspect of courtship.
No account is to be taken except of the actual
money expended or sacrificed.   It is no doubt
true that some countries do permit such an
action so limited.   It is also true that here the
assessment of damages is based ultimately upon
the loss inflicted actually or prospectively, and
that exemplary damage could in principle only
be supported by the obvious circumstances that,
as marriage is a lottery, it is impossible to say
whether the plaintiff may not have lost a prize.
It is equally true that, in cases where there are

I—9

no special circumstances of aggravation, the
sums awarded do in general bear a marked proportion to the amount of money wasted ; but is
it not also the fact that to ignore and to refuse
to take into account the intangible elements of
the courtship is to take a low and unworthy view
of the nature of the contract ?

An engagement is not as a rule the affair of a
moment, broken as soon as made. There is a
period during which the parties belong to one
another in a different but surely in as true a sense
as that in which married people are one. If, as
may well be the case, a man engages the affections
of a girl, courts her until she is a mature woman,
holding off all other suitors and causing her to
regard married life as her destiny, and then without good cause breaks off the engagement, her
loss ought not to be measured, and cannot in
justice be measured, by the amount she has
expended in clothes and household necessaries,
all of which can, in case of need, be put to their
proper use though not in the expected circumstances. She has lost her chances, perhaps
wholly, but in any case to some extent, of finding
a congenial and suitable mate. She has, perhaps insensibly, adapted herself and her thoughts
to the man and his ideas, and will find it difficult,

with attractions perhaps waning, to find another
man. And it has occurred, and will again occur,
that she has neglected, and with apparent reason,
the chance of earning her living and finds herself
forced to seek employment in competition with
younger women and without that skill which she
might have acquired to fit her for more responsible work. During these years, the man has
been in receipt of his income, and his prospects
have improved, and his defection is often due to
the belief that he can by marrying someone else
better his financial and social position. Are these
factors not to be taken into consideration ? Are
the years which a woman truly pledged has wasted
upon one who has proved unworthy to be counted
as nothing ? Is she really in the same position
as in the days when he won her affections ? Is
the shock to her feelings, the sense of disillusion,
and the inevitable distrust of men generally,
to be taken as her whims and fancies, unworthy
of attention ? Surely the position is and must
be that the amount by which her loss is measured
is that which the jury who have heard evidence
of all the circumstances and have given it the
weight which they, with their knowledge and
experience of the world, consider to be right,
appraise as the adequate and proper amount.

The conclusions which are suggested by these considerations may be shortly stated. It is desirable that breach of promise actions should be treated seriously, for they are in the nature of tragedies, not comedies. It is essential that safeguards against the worthless simulator of an expectant bride should be maintained, but no better safeguard exists than in a jury directed by an experienced Judge. The good sense of a jury can safely be relied upon to distinguish between a plaintiff to whom the money loss is an adequate compensation and one who is justly entitled to a more liberal estimate of her loss. And finally, the plaintiff, whether man or woman, who has been the victim of the breach of a solemn contract ought to be left, as in the case of all innocent parties to other contracts which have been broken, to be the sole judge whether to try the hazards of an action or to suffer in silence. Compulsory forgiveness of others' trespasses is not yet a maxim of the law, and it ought not to be made so in that very class of broken contracts where the innocent party may stand in more need of sympathy than in any other.

．．．．．．．．

Not very long ago Mr. Justice McCardie, a very learned and conscientious Judge, after trying an action for breach of promise of marriage, pronounced himself in very definite language as being opposed to the maintenance of this cause of action. A distinguished ex-Home Secretary has recently expressed the same opinion. I differed profoundly from them both ; but, being at that time myself a Judge of Appeal and only in a secondary way a politician, I did not think it proper to express my opinion upon Mr. Justice McCardie's view, unless it should happen to come before me judicially. In such an event I should have expressed my opinion with great clearness. Being now neither a Judge nor, I suppose, even a lawyer, I have the freedom which permits me to make my opinions known on a very important subject of social policy.

I propose now on the whole to discuss the subject rather upon social than upon legal lines, but nevertheless a few legal conclusions are worth the attention of the layman. In the first place, a promise to marry by an infant is voidable by him, and in order to enable the plaintiff to sue there must be proof of a fresh promise after the defendant's majority. In the second place, a plaintiff may sue upon a promise made to him or her while he or she was an infant. In the third place, if nothing is said as to time of performance, the promise is to marry in a reasonable time. In the fourth place, if the plaintiff has lived an immodest life before the date of the promise, the defendant is not bound unless he or she knew of such immodesty when he or she made the promise. In the fifth place, chastity after the promise is a condition subsequent, by the breach of which the defendant is released. In the sixth place, the continued fitness of the defendant for marriage is not such a condition, though this circumstance is of course very relevant in mitigation of damages.

There remains to be made, still confining ourselves to the purely legal sphere, an observation upon the matter of damages. Immorality of the plaintiff, lack of means of the defendant, may very reasonably be urged to reduce the damages. Conversely, if the defendant had seduced the plaintiff by means of his promise, the jury may weigh and give compensation for the social disparagement of the plaintiff.

It only remains, before we dismiss the legal as apart from the social problem that presents itself, to say that under Denman's Act the plaintiff cannot recover a verdict for breach of promise of marriage unless his or her testimony is corroborated by material evidence in support of the promise. The legal points which I have here asserted may on the whole be regarded as well established, though by no means all of them have been affirmed by the House of Lords. In the main, however, I am of opinion that they are unlikely to be disturbed.

I address myself now to certain social questions which are of the utmost interest and importance. It may in the first place be very reasonably asked, in these days when equality of the sexes is so much insisted upon, whether there is any difference between a male plaintiff and a female plaintiff. In law there is none. But it is part of the crazy evolution of our modern social life that we have altogether disregarded, as if we were superior to them, the immutable laws of Nature, and the permanent distinctions of sex. Man is man ; woman is woman. Woman insists on her equal rights in every branch of human life. *Naturam expellas furca, tamen usque recurret.* The more woman insists on her equality, the more man pathetically insists upon her superiority ; and so it happens that, although in the theory of the law a male plaintiff in an action for breach of promise is in precisely the same position as a female plaintiff, in fact he is not. Woman jurors may redress the balance, but I doubt whether they will. I know of no case, for instance, where a masculine plaintiff has gone into the box complaining of seduction. I should myself rather like to meet such a man. I have no means of judging—since I have long since ceased to plead before juries and have never argued before a mixed jury—what degree of support he would be likely to obtain. Yet, if the sexes are really, as we are told, equal for all purposes, why not?

The truth is that the fundamental facts of human nature, despising and destroying (as they always will) the conventions of politics when these are artificial, recognise with complete and immediate sincerity differences which are fundamental. I suppose that in about seventy-five cases out of a hundred women will be normal and feminine. Their destiny in about this proportion—I neglect the unhappy minority—will be to attach themselves to some male who will be responsible for their protection and for their maintenance. Juries, even mixed juries, will not pay the slightest attention to the enactments of Parliament; they will rather fasten upon those elements in human nature and of the sexual relationships which are unalterable by human legislation.

Accordingly, if a male plaintiff appears in the witness-box and explains that he was engaged to be married to a lady of abundant means who has jilted him, he will receive very little consideration. The jury, I believe, unless my experience of juries has become obsolete, will take the rough-and-ready view that it is on the whole the business of a man to support a woman, and not that of a woman to support a man. I have not examined the records of the Courts with any great precision upon this point, but I should greatly doubt whether there has been any case in which a male plaintiff has received heavy damages in such an action. I am not dissentient from the view which in my recollection of the decisions of juries has prevailed, but it provides a somewhat ironical comment upon the claim for equality between the sexes.

I pass now to the case of the woman. The learned Judge to whom I have referred, and for whom I have a great respect, has made it plain that he is opposed to action for breach of promise and regards it as mischievous, whether it proceeds from male or female. I have the misfortune to disagree with his view.

Take, for instance, the case of a woman who became engaged to a man, abandoning her business prospects, never, perhaps, after a two or three years' interval, to be resumed. Why is she to be excluded from the general principles of the Law of Contract ? And take even a more pathetic case : that of a woman who has become engaged at the age of nineteen, has remained under this obligation until she is thirty, and is then abandoned. Her early youth has disappeared ; her chance of procuring a matrimonial establishment for herself and a happy life has been dissipated ; and she is left to face the world in changed conditions, and with no obvious means of securing her own subsistence.

Why is a woman who has sustained this cruel wrong, hardly measurable in damages, who has given all she had in life, her golden, irreplaceable youth, in reliance upon this promise, to be excluded from remedy ? For myself, I make plain my opinion that so incalculable is the valuation of youth that I can hardly measure in terms of damages its pecuniary equivalent. Those twelve years in the life of a woman can never recur ; the man who has wasted them and then left the woman whom he has abandoned to face the world twelve years older, is, in my judgment, a man who ought to pay for the toll he has taken upon a measure commensurate with his own means, and limited only by those means.

A recent case, not without interest, has been widely advertised in the Press. I naturally do not examine it in detail, nor can I even pretend to have read it in detail. But the defence, if I understand the matter aright, was that the defendant was habitually so drunk that he offered marriage to every woman he met. I once had occasion to deliver a judgment upon drunkenness as a defence to crime, which was assented to by all my colleagues, and which might usefully be considered in this context.[1] The defendant in the particular case was able to give coherent, intelligible, and sometimes amusing and ready-witted evidence on his own behalf. If such a man, not being insane, has the misfortune that he cannot resist proposing marriage to every woman he meets, I cannot myself see any reason why he should not pay damages to any woman whom he disappoints. The scale upon which damages are to be assessed will no doubt vary according to the view which the jury takes of the moral value of the plaintiff and the sobriety and seriousness of the defendant. But that a man should be allowed to propose marriage in intelligible and apparently serious language

[1] See Director of Public Prosecutions v. Beard, *Judgments delivered by Lord Chancellor Birkenhead*, pp. 225–39.

to every woman who attracts him, and then, when sued for his necessarily recurrent breaches, reply, " It may be that I promised to marry you, but then I am always drunk," is a claim which I, sitting as a Judge, should sternly repel.

I have not yet examined what I regard as the indisputable justification of an action for breach of promise. This consideration would for ever make it impossible to abolish the action for breach. It almost invariably happens that a woman who is expecting to be married, in reliance upon a promise, will have incurred some actual expenditure. I cannot conceive of any argument which would deny to her the right of recovering a complete indemnity for that which she has spent. And therefore in the real sense the action for breach of promise of marriage can never become obsolete until the Law of Contract itself has become obsolete. And this even in modern conditions, however revolutionary, must take some time.

Summarising, therefore, the views which I have expressed, I reach the following conclusions :

1. The Law of Contract is one and indivisible.

2. A breach of promise to marry is a breach of contract.

3. The breach of such a contract in terms of damages is, in the main, to be measured by the same standards as attend the breach of any other contract.

4. To sweep away this cause of action would be to make an inroad upon the general principles of the Law of Contract, which would be neither justifiable nor tolerable.

.   .   .   .   .

I may perhaps be permitted at this point to make a few observations on a subject which, although it is in law unrelated (though not without analogy) to the question of actions for breach of promise, is nevertheless associated with it in the public mind by a natural process of reasoning. I refer to damages in divorce. The social arguments regarding the propriety of the one may, without undue pressure, be enlisted to a certain degree in respect of the other; indeed similar opinions have been put forward about damages in divorce as have been advanced for and against damages in cases for breach of promise.

In divorce proceedings the most common defence is naturally a denial of the allegations of conjugal misconduct. Here the onus of proof is in all cases imposed upon the petitioner. Other defences fall under two heads : those which, if proved, form an absolute bar to relief ; secondly, those which merely form discretionary bars.

The absolute bars are : connivance, condonation, collusion.

Discretionary bars are : unexplained delay in bringing the petition ; misconduct on the petitioner's part ; desertion by the petitioner ; cruelty, misconduct, or wilful neglect on the part of the petitioner. In the case of neglect and misconduct the court, before using its discretion, will require to be satisfied that they conduced to the respondent's adultery.

This very general statement will enable the layman to apply his mind with the necessary degree of clearness to the special subject matter of this article.

The question of the damages appropriate in divorce proceedings has from time to time been much discussed. Mr. Justice Montague Shearman, a lawyer of very great experience both at the Bar and on the Bench, recently made some most interesting observations upon the subject of the scale and principle upon which damages should be recovered in this class of case. He pointed out in effect that not every peccant spouse was worth anything at all. This observation is undoubtedly true, for many cases come before the Courts in which it is obvious that the man or the woman, as the case may be, is well rid of an inconvenient, bad-tempered, and even immoral incubus. In such a case I hold a jury entitled to give damages expressed even in contemptuous terms.

The object of giving damages in divorce cases is not, in the view of the law, punitive. It has been laid down over and over again that the law only permits a jury to give compensation for the loss which the spouse who brings the petition has sustained. It is evident that this damage is the same whether the co-respondent is a rich man or a poor man. Many Judges, accordingly, in cases of high importance have laid it down that the means of the co-respondent are an utterly irrelevant consideration.

I have myself always thought that this rule, though repeatedly stated in Courts of considerable authority, was laid down too widely. In the first place, every sensible jury, and every sensible Judge in the comparatively rare cases tried without a jury, will be influenced in the amount awarded by the obvious incapacity of the co-respondent (if such be clear) to pay more than a very small sum. To award a sum plainly larger than the co-respondent can conceivably pay is to make it certain that the petitioner will receive nothing, perhaps not even costs. But in such a case it not infrequently happens that a *reasonable* sum can be and is paid. Unless my memory fails me, when I sat as a divorce Judge, I often, in cases which rendered such a view prudent, awarded damages ranging from £5 to £20.

The second exception is more or less reliably admitted, though some slight element of judicial doubt has been thrown upon it. It has been, for instance, laid down that in a case where the co-respondent has used his wealth to effect the seduction of the wife, a larger measure of damages may be allowed. In the terms in which it is laid down I question the theoretic authority of this rule. But the matter is not worth arguing about, for in practice juries will pay regard to such circumstances, and unless their estimate of damages is plainly perverse it cannot be corrected.

What, then, are the main principles upon which damages in these cases are awarded? First, we have seen that we are to ascertain as nearly as we can the actual damage which the petitioner has sustained. But this generalisation requires a closer analysis. The principal justification and ground for damages is naturally the destruction of the matrimonial home. This home has evidently not been destroyed where the spouses have separated before the adultery. In such a case, therefore, a jury might very reasonably measure the damages at a lower rate. But the claim to damages none the less survives, for the loss of the petitioner and the injury to him are evidently not limited to the destruction of his home.

The matter has not, as I have said, been treated in the Courts as being one in which the general behaviour of the co-respondent examined from a moral angle is a strictly relevant consideration. Thus, it is no defence to an action for damages against a co-respondent that he was unaware that his paramour was a married woman. But, in fact, juries in a divorce case have not yet, in my experience, been successfully restrained from giving the fullest weight to the conduct of the co-respondent.

The Court has a very full discretion as to the manner in which the damages shall be disposed of. The practice in this matter seems to me to be correctly summarised in a work upon the subject which I have often found useful : *Browne*

and Watts on Divorce (10th ed., by J. H. Watts),
p. 128 :

" In making orders as to the disposition of
damages the Court will be guided by the circumstances of each individual case. Sometimes
the Court orders them to be paid over to the
petitioner, sometimes that a part be paid to the
petitioner and the remainder settled for the benefit of the children of the marriage (if any), sometimes the whole is ordered to be settled for the
benefit of the children, and sometimes the whole
or a part is even ordered to be settled for the
benefit of the adulterous wife.

" But in every case it is usual to order that
the petitioner's costs—over and above his taxed
costs—shall be first paid out of such damages."

A further rule is laid down which to laymen,
and indeed to some lawyers, has seemed anomalous ; that where the co-respondent dies before
paying the damages, no order for payment can
be enforced against his executor. This is, however, part of a larger principle.

We have seen that, theoretically at least, the
moral conduct of the co-respondent has not been
taken into account in arriving at the measure of
damages, but a similar rule has not been applied
to the case of the petitioner. And so where a

petitioner confessed that he had committed adultery, but established condonation on the part of the wife, the Court, consistently with its general discretionary rule, refused a decree, and therefore excluded him from damages. Enough has perhaps been said to make plain the general principles upon which damages may be awarded in this class of case. Their reasonableness will, on the whole, I believe, recommend them to the common sense of the community. Many men do not care to ask for damages in such a case. This is obviously a matter for their own consideration. The case, indeed, presents some slight analogy to that of those plaintiffs in actions for breach of promise of marriage who, though they may have sustained serious damage, do not care to have it appraised in terms of money by juries.

The modern tendency is, I am inclined to think, not in an ordinary case to award very large sums by way of damages. I myself once, long ago, when at the Bar, obtained a verdict in an undefended case, which, unless my memory plays me false, was for no less a sum than £20,000. It was certainly at least for £10,000. I had completely underrated the generous sympathy of the jury; I employed excessive eloquence; and

I need hardly say that no such amount or anything like it was ever paid. It may indeed be as disadvantageous, for the reasons I have already pointed out, to attain too large a verdict as to be disappointed by one too small.

VI

DIVORCE LAW REFORM

THE problems of divorce in England lead to many differences of opinion, some of the most important of which are irreconcilable. There is, however, one point for which unanimity can be claimed, and that is that the existing law is anomalous and unsatisfactory. Some therefore conclude that divorce ought to be abolished, others again that its scope should be extended.

It is proposed to discuss here the recommendations of the Royal Commission on Divorce which sat for three years before the war under the chairmanship of Lord Gorell, who had occupied the office of President of the Divorce Court, and heard witnesses drawn from all classes of society. These recommendations involve the granting of divorce in five cases which were not admitted by the law in force. Conclusions arrived at by a strong and representative tribunal after a judicial consideration of an immense body of evidence must be admitted to be worthy of the most serious examination, and should not lightly be disregarded.

Before entering upon the detailed examination of the causes thus commended by the Legislature, it is necessary to clear away certain misconceptions and to state concisely certain principles, which may, unless properly understood, confuse the issues and mislead the unwary. It is necessary to understand not merely what is involved by the recommendations but also what is not so involved, for it is of the utmost importance that a social institution like marriage should not be subjected to new legislative recommendations by ignorant support and that defects should not be perpetuated by unreasoning opposition.

First of all, the recommendations do not raise the question whether divorce shall or shall not be allowed at all. As everyone knows, the law definitely and distinctly provides that for certain specified causes, clearly alleged and properly proved, a marriage may be dissolved. The question has been definitely answered once for all, but it is necessary to state the fact, because any suggestion for amendment at once arouses the opposition of those who disagree, not because of the demerit of the particular proposal, but on the ground that marriage is or ought to be indissoluble.

This view is held by many upright and sincere

persons who honestly believe that the indissolubility of marriage is enjoined by God, and further
that it is essential for the welfare of society. A
variant of this principle, based upon the Gospel
of St. Matthew, admits one exception, but only
one—the case of adultery. Adherents of these
beliefs will not be satisfied by any accommoda-
tion or compromise. Any cause of divorce to
the one party or any cause except adultery to
the other is absolutely indefensible. These persons cannot be convinced consistently with their
own faith; they must be overborne. For the
former it is sufficient perhaps to bear in mind that
their rule has been definitely rejected and that
their reasoning has not been accepted by the
vast majority of their fellow-creatures. To answer
those who do admit the exception of adultery but
oppose any extension, it is necessary perhaps to
examine the principle in more detail.

The history of divorce in this country is of
the greatest importance. The principles which
govern marriage and the incidents thereof are
based upon the Canon Law. It is popularly supposed that monogamous marriage is based on the
teaching of the Scriptures, but that is not so. The
only specific reference to marriage with one wife
only is the statement that a person who has more

than one should not be made a bishop. In truth the law of marriage is derived from many sources, mainly the pagan law of Rome as purified and revised by Christian teaching. The Canon Law as settled in the course of the Middle Ages did undoubtedly lay down two great principles : (1) that marriage must be monogamous, and (2) that once a marriage has been validly contracted it remains indissoluble while the parties are still alive.

It is to be regretted that the problem in this country has been complicated by the fact that matters both ecclesiastical and matrimonial were profoundly affected by the matrimonial eccentricities of Henry VIII. He is popularly said to have desired and obtained a divorce, but in truth he aimed at a declaration that his marriage was null on the ground of affinity. Divorce puts an end to a marriage. A decree of nullity declares that there never was a marriage. History, however, has shown that in no period has a man of sufficient importance desired in vain to put an end to his union merely because marriage was indissoluble, and the authorities created by the ecclesiastical law to accommodate the unyielding principle of indissolubility to the relief justly demanded constituted a veritable system of legal fictions whereby a marriage could be declared never to have been a marriage. Nullity has this disadvantage : any children born are made retrospective bastards, a result which is impossible with divorce. From the end of the seventeenth century, divorce in the sense of putting an end to an existing valid marriage has been obtainable by the procedure of promoting a Bill in Parliament founded upon the allegation and proof of adultery. This remedy, judicial in substance though legislative in form, was, however, so costly that admittedly none but the wealthy could have recourse to the procedure. Nevertheless the exercise of such a legislative power put an end in this country to the principle that marriage was indissoluble.

The change brought about by the Matrimonial Causes Act of 1857 was, therefore, merely to transfer divorce jurisdiction from Parliament to the Courts, with the added advantage that the remedy was no longer reserved to people of great means. As the law now stands, omitting certain grounds of a grosser nature, a petition may be presented by a husband or wife praying for a dissolution on the ground that the other party has been guilty of adultery. Beyond all doubt, the system of jurisprudence in this country recognises the principle that marriage is not necessarily indissoluble.

Here one must part company with those who totally reject all idea of divorce, but there remain those who admit the single ground of adultery and refuse to allow any other cause. It is perhaps sufficient to suggest that they too must be held to have had their basic principle rejected, for no one who has read Section 27 of the Act of 1857 can fail to see that adultery is not the only ground now recognised by law. I do not refer expressly to the terms of the section which justify the observation, but they should in fairness ask themselves whether it is the will of God that a man or woman should remain bound to a person who is guilty of the offences set out in the section. There is, however, a broader principle upon which divorce should be justified, for surely the true principle is that marriage ought to be dissoluble on any ground which establishes that in the particular case the fundamental purpose of marriage has been frustrated.

It is astonishing to find men of the greatest experience and ability who can satisfy themselves that adultery alone can justify divorce, and especially to do so on religious grounds. Adultery, after all, is a breach of the carnal implications of marriage. It must be admitted by all right-minded people that the duties of chastity and continence shall be insisted upon. But so to limit the causes of divorce is to ignore the fact that the spiritual and moral aspects of marriage are incomparably more important than the physical side.

What is the explanation? Probably it is nothing more than this, that these high-minded people have not realised that the insistence upon the mere carnal part of marriage is an inheritance, not from the Scriptures, but from the Middle Ages. Just as the mediæval mind could not understand conveyance of land without livery of seisin or dissociate the ownership from the physical custody of chattels, so the common lawyer could not appreciate a marriage without complete intercourse between the spouses. The old law jealously protected the husband's right to custody of his wife—not indeed until 1891 was it made clear that a husband could not seize and imprison his wife. Because we have moved away from these mediæval ideas and the progress of mankind rejects the grosser part as forming the only true essence of marriage, the old notions have ceased to be satisfactory. It is not because people reject the teachings of religion but because they appreciate and apply the true principles of marriage on the spiritual side that the existing rules have been found inadequate.

.   .   .   .   .

It is unfortunately an imperative duty to insist that divorce as a remedy, or advocacy of a particular cause for divorce, is not aimed at the institution of marriage. The remedy is necessary in the higher interests of society, both for its spiritual and moral welfare. The relation of husband and wife is honourable and praise-worthy, but not when it is degraded by including in that relation persons who dishonour and degrade a position which nevertheless they are forced to share with the decent living members of the community, and when they not only share that position but are forbidden to end the rela-tion even with the aim and object of enabling one at least to resume a proper station of society. To insist upon the divine origin and nature of marriage in order to keep in existence unions which have ceased to have anything in common with real marriage but the shadow, and in the name of God to refuse redress to society and the individual, is to fall into the error of those who had to be reminded that the Sabbath was made for man.

The conception of marriage which insists upon the union of flesh obscures the real issues. Further, by laying undue stress on the physical nature of marriage, it underrates and minimises the spiritual side of marriage, and leads to the curious result that the breach of the spiritual obligations of married life, the highest and most important of all, is rejected as a ground of divorce in favour of one which, admittedly sufficient to justify dissolution, is not on the same plane of morality.

From any point of view, religious or social, how can it be good that a marriage which has ceased to be such in everything that really matters shall remain in being simply because it so happens that adultery cannot be proved?

It often happens that the proof is wanting merely through want of means, and, therefore, it is a denial of justice to the poor merely because they are poor. The Court must, while adultery is the ground to be alleged, insist that adultery shall be adequately proved. It could not for a moment listen to a poor woman, for instance, who says, " My husband is at the other end of the world. I am sure he is committing adultery, but my means prevent my obtaining the evidence." A person of means or position can be easily, though sometimes expensively, traced. If there is evidence it is procured, for expense is not a bar in such a case. But it is for those who cannot afford the expense of ascertaining whether there is evidence, quite apart from producing it, that further relief is necessary. Insistence upon adultery, and adultery only, as the ground to be proved may, and does in an increasing degree, produce the same state of affairs as when an Act of Parliament had to be obtained. The remedy is open to all, if they can afford it. This defect cannot be remedied merely by reducing or abolishing the fees payable to the Court. The main expense of legal proceedings is the cost of investigation and the production of evidence, and even if Court, counsel, and solicitor are all made free, the expense where a wife is deserted by a husband who has vanished or in any similar case remains prohibitive.

.   .   .   .   .

The Royal Commission on Divorce issued two Reports. The Majority Report was signed by all but three, though some members made special reservations. The Minority Report was signed by the three dissentients, the Archbishop of York, Sir Lewis Dibden, an eminent ecclesiastical Judge, and the late Sir William Anson.

So far as the two Reports were in substantial agreement, much has been done to carry out the recommendations. A wife can now obtain a decree on the ground of her husband's adultery without alleging any of the additional reasons formerly required. This has practically ended for ever the unsatisfactory form of action for restitution of conjugal rights, whereby a woman who desired to cut short the period of waiting feigned a desire for her husband's return, which was probably the one thing she had ceased to desire.

The revision of the Rules as to Poor Persons has opened the Divorce Court to a new class, the one which is most injured by the infidelity of a spouse. The beginnings of divorce jurisdiction at Assizes have brought some financial relief to those who could ill afford a trial in London, which was until quite recently the invariable rule. Naturally the reduction of expenses has led to a great increase in the number of petitions, but it would be a great injustice to ascribe the increase to a corresponding increase of infidelity among the poor. What has happened is that they can now take advantage of a procedure which was always open to them, but which by reason of expense, might be described as prohibited by everything but the law. The number of those who have taken advantage of the altered conditions proves, not a lowering of the standard of morality, but the urgent need that previously existed for the alteration.

Where the members of the Divorce Commission differed was not as to making divorce available for new classes, but as to admitting new causes of divorce. The majority were so impressed by the evidence given before them that they recommended an extension of the existing law. During the war there was naturally not much opportunity of considering new legislation, but the new conditions that were brought about during the war did accentuate to a marked degree the reasons which brought about the Majority Report. In 1920 Lord Buckmaster introduced in the House of Lords a Bill designed to give effect to the recommendations contained in that Report and prolonged debates were held, during which the divergent views held upon these problems received full expression. It would be impossible to expect unanimity. No social problem, however acute, meets with a solution that is universally accepted. Two points of view emerged from the debates. On one side were those who accept the principle that marriage should be dissoluble when the substratum has wholly disappeared. On the other were two groups, who could unite without inconsistency to oppose the Bill, namely, those who object to divorce for any reason whatsoever, and those who will only admit adultery as the cause. Between these two incompatibles there can be no compromise. One side or the other must prevail, and the minority will submit, not because it is convinced of error, but because it is overborne by the majority.

There is, naturally, no compulsion to seek divorce. However the law be framed, those who object to divorce, whether it be altogether or only on certain grounds, need not seek redress unless they choose. The question is whether persons who would, if the law be altered, claim the relief given by the new provisions, are to be allowed to do so or prevented from obtaining a decree in circumstances which the existing law deems insufficient.

In order to understand and appreciate the problem, it is beyond all doubt essential to know what were the recommendations of the Royal Commission. Those who object to any extension of the law are not much concerned, for whatever be proposed, it is to them anathema. But the general body of the community, who do recognise that the present anomalies of the law call for redress and are prepared to support a proper extension, are vitally interested ; because it does not follow from acceptance of the general proposition that the law should be amended that, therefore, any particular proposal should necessarily be supported. Each must be considered on its own merits in the light of the interests of society as a whole.

Lord Buckmaster's Bill, following the Majority Report, provided for five additional grounds upon which a petition could be presented :

1. Wilful desertion for three years ;
2. Cruelty ;
3. Incurable lunacy of five years' standing ;
4. Habitual drunkenness ; and
5. Imprisonment under a commuted death-sentence.

Each of these must receive detailed examination.

.   .   .   .   .

The proposed new causes cannot be considered as a whole. Each is supported by the general principle already mentioned, viz. that it is right in the interests of society that a marriage shall be dissolved when the marriage has been frustrated. It is not the question of the desire or

whim of the parties to a particular marriage or
of either of them.

1. *Wilful Desertion for Three Years.*—It is
impossible to conceive a graver violation of the
marriage tie than that committed by a man or
woman who wilfully deserts his or her spouse.
The consequences, especially to a deserted wife,
and in the highest degree if she be poor, are a
complete denegation of each and every obligation
solemnly undertaken when the marriage was
contracted. A woman of means can still enjoy
all the advantages that her wealth secures to her.
She can, even if not with the same ease, live in
comfort without her husband's support. She
can in the vast majority of cases discover without
undue difficulty where he has gone, not only
because on the one hand she can afford the necessary investigations, but also for the reason that
men of means cannot easily disappear completely
without also abandoning their resources. She
can, therefore, discover and prove the adultery,
which under the present law will, if it exist,
entitle her to a divorce. But when the deserted
spouse is a poor woman, her position is at once
desperate. She must earn her living, and in
many cases that also of her children. She cannot make the necessary investigations, nor can

she easily guess where her husband may be found. He may be within a few minutes' walk or at the other end of the world. She does not know where he is or what he is doing ; she cannot find out. It is to mock her to say that she can gain her freedom if she can prove adultery, when her lack of means and the pressing need to earn a livelihood conspire to prevent her from even knowing if she can call upon the Court for relief.

It may be objected that the deserter's adultery is assumed too readily. The answer is that the assumption is based on the fact that a person who is so unmindful of the obligations undertaken towards the spouse and any children that may be born is not to be expected to deny the promptings of carnal desire. It is because the committal of adultery is taken as a repudiation of the obligations of matrimony that divorce is thereby justified, but it is a stronger case indeed where all the obligations are repudiated, for there are many cases of casual adultery where the offender does not desire to put an end to his or her married life. Adultery destroys mutual confidence and connubial society ; even more so does wilful and continued desertion. It strikes at the existence of married life and renders impossible what was the very object of the union. In the one case of adultery, the other party is entitled to claim to be released from the marriage ; the case of desertion is a more open, more complete, and less forgivable breach of the very condition upon which alone marriage can exist, and it calls even more insistently, though less publicly, for the same relief.

This leads to the alternative, which is the only suggestion made on the other side, that a separation shall take place, whether by agreement or by judicial decree. The suggestion is no remedy ; it is not even a palliative. Men and women do not marry in order to live a celibate life, and the institution of marriage which is no marriage by reason of separation has no sanction in Holy Writ. That Book lays down the formal principle that it is not good for man to live alone, and separation, unless merely temporary, is a violation of that principle. It is only too certain that the system, adopted from ecclesiastical law but extended by later statutes, aggravates the evil. Where a man or woman in humble circumstances is left deserted, with children to care for, it is almost inevitable that he or she shall form another union. This does not mean that casual or intermittent adultery follows ; on the contrary, it is of the same nature and having the same object as marriage — permanent in intention, monogamous in fact, but perforce adulterous. It is, moreover, not merely without legal sanction, but it is an obstacle to divorce, if it so happen that the necessary evidence becomes available. A petitioner who has committed adultery, no matter what the excuse may be, is no longer entitled to a divorce as of right. The fault must be revealed, and the Judge has then a full and uncontrolled discretion to say whether or not in the circumstances a decree shall be pronounced notwithstanding the petitioner's conduct.

Then, too, arises the terrible problem of the children. A child born of such a union is a bastard, and this must be so if marriage recognised by law is to retain any significance. Most people feel that it is disgraceful to bring illegitimate children into the world. The result is that there are thousands who condemn themselves to sterilisation, though they are in the prime of life and should be contributing towards the supply of new citizens whose birth ensures the continued existence of the Empire. Their spouses deny them the legitimate joys of parenthood. The State affords them no relief ; they and society suffer because, for no fault of theirs, they have been wilfully deserted. They lose the comradeship and discipline of parenthood to save their

children from a stigma which is inevitable under
present conditions. The law gives them no
gleam of hope, and they must despair, because
no effort of theirs can restore or replace a union
which has been deliberately shipwrecked by the
other party, who no doubt lives untrammelled
by any consideration of decency or by any of the
obligations that rest equally upon him. The
punishment falls upon the innocent in order to
ensure the sacred principle that a marriage which
has become no marriage shall nevertheless be
upheld.

Reference is often made to the experience of
other countries. It is suggested that to admit
desertion would, if such experience be of value,
result in grave moral degeneration. Indeed it
has been suggested that it would in effect amount
to divorce by mutual consent. It is, however,
fortunate that an example lies at our doors.
Since 1573 Scotland has admitted desertion as a
ground for divorce, and her experience of 350
years amply disproves the suggestion that grave
evil will come upon this country. Lord Salvesen,
a Scottish Judge of the greatest authority and
experience, told the Commission that " there
appears to be nothing to justify the fears of those
who fear the effect of divorce being granted for

desertion. On the contrary, while these decrees on the ground of desertion have no doubt remedied very serious grievances, no abuse of this right appears to exist, nor does there seem any reason to suppose that any abuse of it would be found in England."

It is easy, no doubt, to collect particular instances from abroad of decrees granted for inadequate causes or upon insufficient evidence. The lax administration of justice, wherever and whenever it occurs, is an unmitigated evil both to society and to individuals, and it is not fair argument to cite them in this connection. They are not typical of justice here, and to suppose that English Judges will altogether change their methods of thought merely because wilful desertion is made a cause for divorce is opposed to all reason and all experience. Judges would continue to decide cases in the altered law in the same manner and require the same proof as they do at present.

Nor would such an amendment of the law lead to divorce by mutual agreement, even assuming the utmost desire for a collusive decree. No doubt married people will adopt fraudulent and collusive devices to deceive the Court, but no one with the slightest experience will be ignorant of cases in which collusion is suspected or of the difficulty of bringing it home to the offenders or of the fact that, if collusion is practised, it will be foolish to pretend to have wilfully deserted the petitioner for three years, when to pretend to have committed adultery yesterday will bring about the same result more quickly and with less risk of detection. Desertion cannot give more scope for collusion.

2. Desertion, the most frequent of the new grounds put forward, implies the loss of affection, even if the affection be not transferred to another, and also the failure to realise or fulfil the obligations of married life.   The second cause, *Cruelty*, implies that the victim's spouse—one may assume that the aggressor is almost always the husband in such cases—remains at the house and more or less assists to maintain it.   The wife has the alternative to remain and be tortured, or to go away and live celibate and alone.   Married life in any sense that is worthy of the name is impossible.   No one would suggest that such a wife should remain with a man who has proved himself a brute.   The only difference of opinion is whether such a union is so sacred that it must at any cost to the victim remain undissolved.

The opposition to this amendment naturally

does not palliate the evil. Maintenance of the
state of marriage connotes cohabitation, but no
one would be so temerarious as to hint that a
wife ought in such a case to remain with her
husband. That aspect of the question is neglected
for the more subtle point that cruelty is indefinite
—difficult to define, and hard to describe—and
that to admit such a reason would be to raise
problems never easy and often insoluble. This
reasoning assumes that redress should not be
given, merely because the solution is difficult.
It is not a characteristic of English Judges to
shirk any difficulty which justice requires them to
face. But it may well be questioned whether
cruelty is so difficult to define or, once defined, so
impossible to apply to particular facts.

Until 1923 cruelty as well as desertion was
one of those accessory conditions which must
have been alleged and proved by a woman
petitioner. There is, accordingly, ample authority
as to what the Courts will hold to constitute
cruelty. A dependable definition is " such conduct by one married person to the other party to
the marriage as makes it unsafe, having regard
to the risk of life, limb, or health, bodily or mental,
for the latter to continue to live with the former."
The Commission proposed to add two further

matters : (*a*) where one party of the marriage has wilfully or negligently infected the other with venereal disease, and (*b*) where the husband has compelled the wife to submit to prostitution. The difficulty of defining cruelty and of applying the definition to particular cases was successfully overcome during the period 1857–1923, and the difficulty is not increased where the cruelty alleged is the only issue instead of being one of two issues. Opponents of this reform are driven to prescribe the remedy of judicial separation, the evils of which have already been described.

3. *Incurable Lunacy of Five Years' Standing.*— This proposal was not accepted by the majority as unhesitatingly as the two former. Mrs. Pennant, for example, expressed herself in doubt, because, if habitual insanity was to be sufficient, what was to be done with cases of recurrent insanity where the patient may in the intervals of treatment make himself or herself responsible for bringing children into the world ? This objection is not valid, because it really amounts to a suggestion that the line will be drawn too narrowly, not that the proposed ground ought not to be allowed. Thousands are tied for life to lunatics, and it is no answer to allege, in many cases with perfect truth, that the insanity is due

to no fault of the lunatic. It merely confuses the issue. Adultery, which is the allegation required at present to be made, involves not merely the real vital issue, whether for reasons of social policy a marriage shall be declared to be at an end, but also the moral issue of blame ; but this is due to the accident of circumstances. Divorce is allowed in the interests of society, and it is also a valid principle of justice that no one shall be heard to allege his own default or wrong-doing, but it is not essential that the cause of divorce shall involve or imply the moral turpitude of the respondent. The point is the interest of society, and it is not to the public welfare that utter unsuitability for the married state, whether the cause be moral, mental, or physical, should not involve the same consequences. A lunatic cannot marry ; why should a lunatic be allowed to continue to be married merely because the lunacy supervened ?

In innumerable instances the lunatic is incapable of realising that he or she is married, but nevertheless it is seriously argued that the other spouse must remain tied for life to one who is unconscious even that he or she is married. It is not as though such insanity is inconsistent with longevity. Many lunatics live to great ages.

To avoid certain evils which may be anticipated, it was proposed that such insanity should not be permitted to be the ground of a petition if the respondent, being a male, was over sixty, or, being a female, over fifty. This limitation is open to criticism, for it is by no means uncommon to find a man over that age married to a young wife ; but probably it is safe to assume that a man of sixty would not have remained sane so long and have married so late that his wife could be youthful at the date of claiming relief. Probably the limitation would only exclude those who have accepted the position for many years and then for some reason have changed their minds.

What has to be borne in mind is the more usual case where in the early years of marriage, sometimes even almost before it has begun, one of the parties is found to be insane and proves to be incurable. Thus the prospect of the union and its whole purpose are irretrievably blasted, and there is no purpose, social or moral, which can be served by maintaining in law the continuance of a marriage which has ceased in fact. The evils which flow from desertion are equally manifest in the case of lunacy, and the remedy ought and must be the same. This is not to deny or weaken the claim of the lunatic that his or her material welfare and comfort shall be secured so far as means or the prospect of means allow, but this does not involve the conclusion that a patient who does not know or care for the presence of his spouse shall bring about the sacrifice of the whole life of the other. There is no need to offer sacrifice at the altar of an unmeaning conjugal fidelity in opposition to the true interests of society.

4. *Habitual Drunkenness.*—The proposal was that habitual drunkenness should enable the other spouse to obtain a separation and then, if after the lapse of three years the offender remains confirmed in his beastliness, an application could be made for divorce. Mrs. Pennant again doubted, because she felt that a woman might try to redeem her husband. Experience has shown that the great majority of the women who now apply for separation orders in circumstances mainly due to their husband's drunken habits have already exhausted every effort to redeem them. The social aspect of drunkenness which superficially renders it excusable is responsible for the fact that its menace to society is not fully appreciated. As the Commission said, " Such inebriety " (i.e. habitual drunkenness) " carries with it loss of interest in surroundings, loss of

self-respect, neglect of duty, personal uncleanli-
ness, neglect of children, violence, delusions of
suspicion, a tendency to indecent behaviour,
and a general state which makes companionship
impossible. In the case of a drunken husband,
the physical pain of brute force is often added to
the mental and moral injury he inflicts upon his
wife ; moreover he has power to reduce himself
and those dependent upon him to penury. In
the case of a drunken wife, neglect of home
duties and of the care of the children . . . and
many attendant evils produce a most deplorable
state of affairs. In both cases the ruin of the
children can be traced to the evil parental
example."

Drunkenness notoriously leads to slackening
of the moral fibres. The drunkard who at first
displays abnormal sexual activity tends, as his
degradation continues, to abnormal manifesta-
tions of sex. The children born before the
habit was formed are subjected to the fitful
violence and perpetual shame of a drunken parent,
but those who are begotten during the stages of
degeneration may develop also all the varieties
of abnormality which are the despair of our
asylums and workhouses. Drunkenness is the
most powerful auxiliary of crime, for the weaken-

ing of self-control gives full play to all the temptations which lead man to commit crime.

The present system condemns the other party to livelong degradation, deepened perhaps by the birth of unwholesome children, or to sterile isolation. A person so living without hope of mercy from the law, may be induced by despair to bring about that separation by death, which alone now can end the marriage. There can be no valid reason why a drunken sot shall remain married at the expense of the other spouse.

5. *Imprisonment under a commuted Death-sentence.*—In such a case, the State has decided that the offender's life is forfeit. For mercy's sake his life is spared, but he is removed from the society of mankind. Had the sentence of the law remained, the offender's marriage would necessarily have ended, and the other party could have married again. The State, having spared the offender's life without letting him go free, has deprived the wife (or husband) of the spouse and also of release from the marriage which in effect it has determined. When the law takes away the whole basis of a marriage, the least it can do is to give the other party the right to put an end to it, if so minded. It is objected that the number affected is small, and indeed the average at any

time is somewhat less than a hundred, but the law should redress wrongs even if one person alone is injured. To deny justice because the injured are few is to measure it by detestable scales.

. . . . .

The five grounds have now been set out and explained. It remains to deal with the amendments put forward regarding the law of nullity, which, it will be remembered, differs from divorce in that it does not put an end to a marriage but declares that there never was a marriage at all. One relates to the dreadful case of a man who marries a woman only to discover that she was pregnant by another man at the time. As the law now stands, the husband cannot repudiate the marriage, nor is there any supervening cause which would entitle him to a divorce. It is a horrible fate to be condemned to a union which has been ruined at the very outset by the imminent birth of a bastard masquerading as the first born. It is proposed to give the husband in such a case the right to a decree of nullity.

A further improvement which is suggested, omitting here certain amendments which do not make very material differences, is to enable a marriage to be annulled if it be proved that either party was at the date of the marriage in a state

I—12

of mental unsoundness which becomes definite
within six months, or was then subject to recurrent fits of insanity or epilepsy, or suffering from
venereal disease in a communicable form, but
under condition that the petitioner comes to the
court for relief before intercourse has taken
place and within one year of the marriage. It
can hardly be contended that any of these persons
are fit for marriage at the time, and it will be
noticed that the nullity is not a permanent dis-
qualification. There is nothing to prevent a
subsequent valid marriage, if the party in question can and does recover from the disability.

So far the objections to the recommendations
which have been considered have been those
based upon a disinclination or refusal to admit
that there is sufficient reason for adopting them.
It is necessary to add some remarks upon another
class of objection, viz. that they do not go far
enough. Even conceding that such be the fact,
it affords no reason not to support the proposals.
They are distinguished from all others in that
they are put forward on the authority of a distinguished body of persons drawn from all
classes of the community after a judicial consideration of evidence, both for and against, of persons
who are or may be affected and of others who,

not being personally affected, have such experience of social conditions that their opinion was worthy of consideration. Other and extended proposals may be found hereafter to be justified, but at present they have not the support which the present proposals have. There is consequently not the same assurance that they are needed in the interest of society. Indeed, the fact that they have not been endorsed by the Majority Report tends to show that there may be some evil consequences to society; but this is not the case with the recommendations which I have passed under review.

It must be emphasised that there is here no countenance of divorce by mutual consent. The interests of society both now and in the future are paramount. It is to further the general welfare that an end should be put to unions which have ceased to be true marriages and which merely exist to plunge one or both of the parties in misery and grief. But it is not conducive to the best interests of the nation that marriages shall be ended merely because the parties, being otherwise fit and capable, desire to part; nor is it, in the long run, to their own advantage. The whim or caprice of the individual cannot be admitted to the status of a rule of social law.

The grave objections to the only suggested alternative of separation have been already stated. It must be reiterated that the existence of divorce does not compel anyone to apply for a decree ; nor does the lawfulness of a fresh union force any one to contract one. Nevertheless, it must be borne in mind that separation without divorce encourages and in certain cases compels the contracting of fresh unions outside the law, and that the unlawfulness of such unions may (and does in countless cases) cause the parties to sterilise themselves and thus to do the State a grave injury. Those who refuse to admit divorce will, of course, remain unmoved by these considerations.

There is also the suggestion that divorce ignores the claims of the children. Nothing is further from the truth. Any proposal to which such a criticism could legitimately be applied would be utterly unworthy of support. The children are entitled to the most serious consideration, even more than are the parties immediately concerned. It is because the lot of the children will be happier and brighter that support is claimed. Children of an existing marriage will thereby be withdrawn from contact with a parent who has by moral or physical taint rendered himself or herself unfit for the responsibility of marriage. They will be freed from the influence of squalor and immorality, from drunkenness, cruelty, and degenerate brutality, and be given a chance to develop both mind and body in homes where they at least can enjoy happiness and security. It cannot be good for a child to grow up in a home where either the father or the mother is living in open adultery and where its natural brothers and sisters incur the stigma of illegitimacy. And these brothers and sisters, the offspring of substitute unions, must also be considered. Their birth is not a source of pride ; they are the ever-present reminder that they are the offspring of an unhallowed union and share their fate with children born of casual and unreflecting immorality. Yet the latter are regarded with more indulgence than those born of a union compelled by circumstances and having all the characteristics of marriage but the sanctions of the law. Then too there are the children, so urgently due to the nation, who are denied existence as a sacrifice to the law. Are they to be ignored ?

The main justification for an extension of divorce is the state of matrimony itself. Under the law as it now stands the honourable matron shares the name of wife with the woman who has

182   DIVORCE LAW REFORM

deserted or disgraced her husband. The husband who governs a happy and united household has the same position in the eye of the law as the vagrant or drunkard who contemns a status which he does not understand but disgraces by his acts. The existence of degraded and frustrated marriages is a menace to society, for they tend to lower the estimation in which married people are justly held and also to encourage the frame of mind which excuses irregularities because the law denies a lawful union. Such abortive marriages should by divorce be utterly ended, so that the parties should be enabled to enter into honourable and open alliances. This would thus remove the just excuse which may now exist for extra-matrimonial establishments and would thereby expose those who form them without such excuse to the condemnation that they rightly incur. The formation of a healthier and more instructed public opinion must tend to raise the general standard of morality and thus also improve the status of matrimony. Results such as these are worth striving for, the more so because the law will, by them, be brought more into accord with the facts and needs of our social life.

. . . .

It is fifteen years since the Majority Report

of Lord Gorell's Commission, and nothing has been done to carry out its recommendations except the beginnings of divorce jurisdictions at Assizes and the fact that a wife can now obtain a decree on the ground of her husband's adultery without alleging any of the additional reasons formerly required. The essential recommendation of the Royal Commission—the extension of the grounds of divorce—has been left untouched, and unless the reformers speak out the issue may be neglected for a generation, to the grave detriment of the body politic.

The difficulty is to get any kind of straight issue with the opponents of Divorce Law Reform. The opposition to reform comes in reality from a comparatively small group of opinion which holds very extreme, or at best very literal, views as to what can be permitted in this direction by the Church or by the narrower interpretation of the Scriptures. And this group is very influential compared with its numbers in both Houses of Parliament. But if it was apparent to the common-sense view of the great mass of the nation that all advance was being held up by people who in a certain interpretation of the Scriptures deny divorce altogether, and would either repeal the Act of 1857 or will never agree to its extension, the public would very soon make a clean sweep of the obstructionists.

The opposition itself is well aware of this fact. In consequence it camouflages a resistance ecclesiastical and mediæval in origin by the pretence that it is actuated by motives based on a social reason. And this is true both of Bishops and pious laymen, who press intellectual honesty to the point where it becomes pure casuistry. They assume for the purpose a vice of Rationalism which they do not possess.

There are exceptions who cling to intellectual honesty. A conspicuous one was Lord Braye, who in the Second Reading debate of Lord Buckmaster's Bill (which embodied the Majority proposals) in the House of Lords, in March 1920, expressed the view of the Roman Catholic Church towards divorce on any ground whatever. " It seems to me," he said, " a waste of time to consider any part or portion of this Bill when you absolutely disagree with the principle and when you absolutely deny the basis of the whole structure of the Bill." These are the words of an outspokenness which might have been imitated with advantage by subsequent speakers on the anti-reform side.

The Archbishop of York, on the other hand,

in one of the most adroit speeches I have ever heard, either in Parliament or at the Bar, managed to transfer his opposition to Lord Buckmaster's Bill from the position assumed by Lord Braye to the attitude of those who accepted adultery as a cause, but the only cause, of divorce, and, finally, to that of a man who had really no ecclesiastical prejudice on the matter at all, but just thought that the measure was socially inexpedient. His argument went through three phases, all gliding imperceptibly into one another.

1. " I ought to say I think in candour that to me personally the conception of marriage as dissoluble only by death is the conception which answers to the mind and teaching of the Divine Head and Founder."

This can only mean that all divorce is wrong. What, then, is the good of discussing the details of Lord Buckmaster's Bill ?

2. The Archbishop moved one step from this fundamental position by admitting that there was a possible exception authorised by our Lord, and embodied in the Act of 1857. He denied that this question was before the House, so that no one knows to this day whether he approves of divorce for adultery or not. But his statement was so calculated as to carry the votes both

of those who believed that no grounds justified divorce or that one ground justified it.   The entire ecclesiastical vote was therefore in his pocket by the time he was halfway through his speech.

3. The Most Reverend Prelate then shifted his entire ground again. " After all, I admit that civil legislation cannot persistently sustain itself upon a level which the public opinion of the community is unable to reach.   Therefore, it is not upon the grounds of religious authority, but upon the grounds of public welfare that I wish to discuss this matter."

After that it follows naturally enough that those who care only about social welfare and not about the Church of Christ at all must find themselves, on a mere rational examination of the facts of Divorce Reform, opposed to Lord Buckmaster's Bill.   The Most Reverend Prelate's noble army was thus recruited of the people who believe in St. Matthew, of those who decline to accept the exception of St. Matthew, and of those opponents of divorce who are asked by the Archbishop not to trouble about the Gospel view at all.   The goats are thereby marshalled into the same lobby with the sheep.

Lord Phillimore, who also spoke on this occasion, was unable to keep up this high level of casuistry.

He was all against the Divorce Bill of 1857. "And, if I could, I would go back to the state which existed before, and I would have no divorce at all." But after this outburst of frankness comes the inevitable twist. "I am not speaking merely as a Christian, and as a believer and as a member of the Church of England; I am looking at the matter from the point of view of the social order." It is the children of divorced parties whose condition concerns Lord Phillimore, who does not believe in divorce at all on purely religious ground. It is curious that no one either in the Lords or the Commons rose in his place and said: "I disbelieve in divorce on religious grounds, but I recognise that the social argument is against me." It is impossible, I suppose, to expect so much candour even in Israel.

After a great struggle in Committee in the Lords the Bill was passed with a few minor amendments. But on April 14, 1920, the House of Commons passed a hostile amendment to the principle of the Bill, on the motion of Mr. Ronald McNeill. The Whips were not put on, the House was a small one, and there voted for the principles of the Bill 91, and against 134. There was a refreshing lack of ecclesiastical cant in the debate.

But it produced one surprise. Lady Astor opposed
the extension of the grounds of divorce. " I am
not," she said, " convinced that making divorce
easy makes happy marriages more possible."

In the meantime a meeting was held to
denounce Lord Buckmaster's Bill at the Caxton
Hall. That eminent democrat, the Duke of
Northumberland, denounced the House of Lords
for passing a measure in defiance of popular
opinion. The democracy was to compel the
House of Commons to override the opinion of the
Peers. Lord Buckmaster's Bill was a measure
propounded by the vicious rich to be imposed
on the virtuous poor. I wonder how the *Morning
Post* regarded this strange doctrine. I have
generally been inclined to hold the *Morning Post*
view that, when it comes to matters of social
legislation which affects the intimate lives of the
people, the Lords are apt to take a more sensible
standpoint than the Commons, because they
have more knowledge and greater sympathy.
But the Duke of Northumberland apparently
does not agree.

The late Father Bernard Vaughan, who
followed, put the Catholic view at its highest.
The public should refuse Lord Buckmaster's Bill
because it legitimised polygamy, sanctioned

licensed prostitution, and turned the country into a stockyard. According to this view this country has been a modified stockyard ever since 1857, and the late Lord Gorell and the very eminent and respectable members of Society who signed the Majority Report are in favour of every kind of public immorality. The Archbishop of York, like Catiline, must be judged by his friends.

.   .   .   .   .

I believe that all these additional grounds for divorce embodied in Lord Buckmaster's Bill can be supported on the grounds of individual justice, public expediency, and State policy. But if anyone answers me, as he might do quite fairly, that what might be expedient for the State is forbidden by the Church, and that between these two positions any man's conscience may be placed in a difficulty, I would advise him to study the theology of the question. He will find that the attitude taken up by the Archbishops in the House of Lords is disputed by some of the greatest authorities within the Anglican Church. Professor Sanday considered that " our Lord's words, however reported, express a moral idea rather than a positive rule, that they did not exclude the possibility of exception, stated in the New Testament, that is, the cause of adultery."

The late Dean Rashdall, of Carlisle, an eminent theologian and metaphysician, put forward in *The Times* (May 1920) the view that the sayings of Christ about non-resistance to evil men, not swearing oaths, and divorce " express an ideal which a Christian society should, as far as possible, seek to realise—but which require considerable qualification in practice." A Bishop, for instance, has to swear an oath on taking office—and Christian men have been known to resist Germans forcibly. The Dean goes on : " In an ideal society there would be no divorce, because there would be no adultery, no desertion, no cruelty, no drunkenness. The ideal of marriage is the lifelong union of two persons—when through the fault of one of the parties such an ideal union has become impossible, the question arises which is the less of two evils, the permission of re-marriage or the compulsory unhappiness of both parties. That is a question upon which our Lord's explicit teaching contains no express guidance."

Where Professor Sanday differs from the Archbishop of Canterbury and Dr. Rashdall from the Archbishop of York, a layman may perhaps be allowed to follow the dictates of justice and common sense.

The essential and urging reason for Divorce Reform in the sense indicated by the Majority Report and Lord Buckmaster's Bill, is that the thought of the mass of the community has marched past, not only the mediæval conception of marriage as an indestructible sacrament, but even the provisions of the Divorce Bill of 1857. The law of the land in this respect is becoming more and more at variance with the opinion of the people. And when this happens, all kinds of undesirable and even dangerous results ensue. Lord Eldon wept on the Woolsack when, because juries would no longer convict, hanging for a forty-shilling theft was abolished. The Duke of Wellington denied to the end of his days that discipline in the Army could be preserved without flogging. What would the law or the Army be like to-day if the obstructionists had not been compelled to yield to the common sense and the common humanity of the nation? In so far as the Bishops are using their public position—not their private right to direct the conscience of their flock—to obstruct Divorce Law Reform they must rank with Eldon or Wellington. That is to say, that if they succeeded they would damage the institution of marriage in this country as much as Eldon would have brought the law into contempt and Wellington have made the Army impossible.

Two signs that society will no longer recognise the old ecclesiastic prohibition in this issue— even as modified by the State in 1857—are apparent, one among the rich and one among the poor.

The poor are by nature frightfully respectable. For generations a suggestion about the absence of marriage lines has been the last imaginable insult. But the fact is, as social workers will testify, that nowadays where a husband or a wife has simply vanished into the blue for years on end, and the deserted party finally settles down into a new union, which though technically irregular is morally that of a marriage relation, the neighbours say nothing at all. They know perfectly well that the absconding party is one against whom any amount of acts warranting divorce could be proved, but that the poor cannot afford tracing and proof. They therefore sniff both at the law and the Church and substitute public opinion for it. And this is very bad for both institutions affected and for the body politic as a whole. How such a state of affairs advances the sanctity of the marriage tie I cannot conceive. The refusal to grant divorce for deliberate desertion does not prevent adultery : it merely makes the people condone or approve it.

The symptom among the rich is a different one. It is the immense spread of what is known as the collusive divorce. For thirty or forty or even fifty years after the Act of 1857 actions for divorce were fought desperately, both by respondent and co-respondent. A woman's reputation and even a man's social existence were destroyed by condemnation in either rôle. The greatness of Parnell, the brilliant hopes entertained for Charles Dilke, did not save them from absolute ruin for being condemned of this offence. But the conditions, both of public and private life, have changed demonstrably since their days. It is not many years ago since a well-known member of Parliament, a war-hero, and subsequently a Minister of the Crown, openly boasted in the lobby of the House of Commons that, though a Judge had been compelled to grant his wife a decree of divorce against him on the ground of adultery, he was, for reasons well known to those to whom he spoke, absolutely innocent.

The hon. and gallant member in question

I—13

never suffered either personally or politically
from the judgment. Why not ? Because the
force of social opinion has changed its direction
in these matters since the 1890's. It has altered
so far that it has made a farce of the Law in too
many instances—as Divorce Court Judges know
only too well.

The present view among the intellectual and
well-to-do is in the main that there are far more
serious grounds for divorce than adultery, but
that, if the law is so foolish as to make that act
a preliminary condition to divorce, then an
adultery, real or pretended, must take place.
The husband, being the least liable to social
blame, shoulders, as a rule, the onus of the fault,
and, it may be added, suffers very little for his
chivalry. Is this a satisfactory state of affairs ?
I do not believe for a moment that the present
generation treat the question of adultery any less
seriously than their predecessors of the nineteenth century. The present age is simply compelled to assume a vice, though it has it not,
because the law under a perverted ecclesiastical
influence will give it no other form of relief. And
society does not condemn the figment.

It is therefore clear that the social conditions
which made the Act of 1857 effective have

vanished. The poor ignore it in one way and the rich evade it in another. The law must therefore be brought into some relation with the conscience of the people, or disastrous consequences will ensue. For if certain people do things with the excuse of the intolerance of the law, why should others not do it without that excuse?

Such is the state of affairs to which the Bishops and the pious laymen in Parliament have reduced the law of England on marriage by persistent refusal to accept the reasonable proposals of the Majority Report of the Divorce Law Commission of 1912. Their mental position is a curious one. They are not legislating for their own flock. It is open to the Church of England to refuse membership to those who decline to accept its views on divorce. Since the repeal of the Test Acts the Church is a voluntary association with no civic disabilities attaching to a citizen who declines membership. No member of the Church of England need sue for a divorce nor need re-marry if divorced. All that the Bishops and their lay retainers in the Houses are doing is to compel other people to live up to standards which they do not accept. In this way the Bishops are violently constraining the consciences of people who do not agree with them. In taking up this

attitude they are serving no useful purpose whatever. They are merely encouraging the poor to
disregard the marriage tie and the rich to laugh at
the law.

The Church of Rome is perfectly logical in
this matter. It has no temporal authority. It
has no vote on the divorce laws of France or
Italy. It denies the right of divorce entirely,
though it has in practice made certain exceptions,
chiefly, I suspect, for the rich and powerful, on
the ground of nullity.

If a Roman Catholic will not conform, he for-
feits the benefits of his Church. That is right
and reasonable. If a member of the Church of
England will not conform on the divorce issue,
the Archbishops can, if they are so minded, compel
him to forfeit communion with his Church.
That, again, is right and reasonable. But why
should the Archbishops and their lay friends in
the Houses of Lords and Commons have the right
to refuse relief in divorce cases to men of different
communions who do not accept their views at all?
Their action in this matter is nothing else than a
minority tyranny which eases one conscience by
outraging two others.

VII

THE King's Proctor is well known to the public as the official who intervenes in divorce cases in order to prevent a divorce decree being made absolute. The nature of his work renders him peculiarly liable to criticism which is not usually well informed. Some is aimed at the system itself, and part, which is aimed at a particular phase of his activities, where parties who have made a shipwreck of their matrimonial life are prevented from making a fresh start, is frequently made without due regard to the nature of his duties. These are onerous and unpleasant, calling for the display of much tact and discretion. Few people outside the comparatively narrow circle of Divorce Court practitioners are aware of the precautions, both statutory and administrative, devised to secure that the acts of the King's Proctor shall not be oppressive, or of the care which is taken not to launch charges against petitioners without some solid reason for them.

A full explanation of the office and its duties will go far to remove existing misapprehensions and to secure that criticism shall be directed to the right quarter. It is useless to grumble at the King's Proctor for doing what he is bound to do. If his duty in that respect is believed to conflict with public interests, then it is the system that should be attacked.

The duties of the King's Proctor in matrimonial causes are due to conditions which are hardly ever present in ordinary civil litigation. In actions it may as a rule be assumed that the parties may safely be left to look after their own interests ; collusion, therefore, is in such cases practically unknown. In divorce causes, on the other hand, so long as the grounds for divorce are strictly limited and defined, there must always be many occasions when both parties urgently desire that a decree should be made and bend their energies to obtain that result. There must also be many persons who are not entitled to divorce but desire it so intensely that they will stop short at nothing to secure what they, but not the law, consider to be their due. It follows, therefore, that if the policy of the law is to be upheld, some system must exist to secure that divorce shall only be available for persons really entitled to that relief in accordance with the law. There was no such provision in the Matrimonial Causes Act, 1857, which created the modern law of divorce, but three years later provision was made with that object by the amending Act of 1860.

The safeguards are :

First, that no decree for divorce is given by default.

Secondly, that no decree is made absolute in the first instance.

There is a period between a decision in the petitioner's favour and the moment when it comes into full operation ; and during that period anyone, not merely the King's Proctor, may intervene.

The first safeguard operates at the time the petition comes on for hearing. Then the petitioner must prove his or her case to the satisfaction of the Court, and it by no means follows that the Court will be satisfied. In civil actions, speaking generally, a defendant may choose not to defend, and judgment will go against him by default. Even in criminal trials the accused can plead guilty, and his plea will obviate any need to call witnesses. In divorce causes, on the other hand, default of defence will not prevent proof. Undefended cases are put in a separate list, and, though

taken rapidly, are not heard carelessly ; so that
unless a case is made out the petition will be dis-
missed. The second safeguard is peculiarly the
province of the King's Proctor ; but, as his
functions are not limited to intervention, it is
better first to describe the office and its organisation, and then to discuss in some detail the duties
which are cast upon him.

The name " Proctor " is unfamiliar to those
who take no interest in the life of their immediate
forbears ; but less than one hundred years ago
the institution of Proctors seemed destined to
last for many years, as it had done for some
hundreds of years before. A Proctor was an
officer of the old ecclesiastical Courts who fulfilled the duties of an attorney in the Common
Law Courts or of a solicitor in the Court of Chancery. His position was not quite identical with
theirs ; but the differences are immaterial for the
present purpose. He instructed counsel, who
were styled Advocates and belonged to Doctors'
Commons, a society similar to but distinct from
the Inns of Court. Neither the Proctor nor the
Advocate practised, or had any right to practise,
in the Courts of Common Law or of Chancery,
but, on the other hand, until the Victorian
changes they had a monopoly of the work in

their own Courts. The Proctor who acted for the interests of the Crown was the King's Proctor and the Advocate retained in the same interest was styled the King's Advocate.

Now all have disappeared, but the office of King's Proctor has been maintained because of the statutory duties cast upon him by the Act of 1860. The Treasury Solicitor is now always appointed King's Proctor, but the offices are distinct and there is a separate staff. During the war the King's Proctor acted for the Crown in prize cases, but the staff in prize work was separate from the staff for divorce work, and in prize cases the King's Proctor was for distinctive reasons given his alternative name—His Majesty's Procurator-General. The King's Proctor is therefore the Crown solicitor in divorce cases.

His statutory duties were conferred on him in the following way. The Matrimonial Causes Act, 1857, abolished the jurisdiction of ecclesiastical Courts in matters matrimonial, and vested it in a new Court, which has been merged in the Probate, Divorce, and Admiralty Division of the High Court. Before that Act, divorce in the sense of a dissolution of marriage was only possible if a private Act of Parliament could be obtained. Although such an Act was granted after a hearing before the Lords as a kind of judicial remedy, it was in itself, and by reason of the necessary preliminary proceedings, so expensive as to be out of question for persons even of considerable means. The ecclesiastical Courts had power to declare a marriage null and void where the ceremony was invalid or there was a defect in the capacity of the parties, but their decree of divorce *a mensa et thoro* was merely the modern judicial separation. The Act of 1857 enabled the new Court to grant decrees of divorce—that is, of dissolution of an existing valid marriage—but only in certain cases.

The causes, though they have been altered, as notably by the Act of 1923, which enables a wife to obtain a divorce for her husband's adultery alone, have always been rigidly limited. The Court, however, even when the ground alleged has been proved, must not grant a decree where there has been collusion or connivance at or condonation of the matrimonial offence; and it is empowered to refuse to grant relief where the petitioner is guilty either of adultery, or of unreasonable delay, or of cruelty, or of desertion, or wilful separation before the adultery alleged, or of wilful neglect or misconduct which conduced to the adultery.

At first the Court gave the desired relief when

giving the decision, but a jurisdiction so swift evidently enabled petitioners to obtain decrees to which they were not entitled; further powers therefore were given by the Act of 1860 already referred to. By sections of this Act the Court was empowered in every case of a petition for dissolution of marriage to direct, if it thought fit, that the papers should be sent to the King's Proctor, whose duty it was made, under the direction of the Attorney-General, to instruct counsel. The object was to enable the Court to have any point adequately argued on both sides. In an undefended case or if a point of importance arises in a defended case which is such that the parties ought not in fairness to bear the burden of investigating and deciding the question, the power may be extremely useful. It is, however, sparingly used, and only in cases where it is essential in the interests of justice.

One example is the recent case of Gaskill *v.* Gaskill. There the only evidence of adultery which could be relied on was that the respondent gave birth to a child 331 days after the husband left this oountry upon active service. If he could not possibly have been the father, the inference of misconduct became irresistible, but not other- wise. The case called for the assistance of the greatest experts in gynæcology, and I myself, sitting at *Nisi Prius*, asked that the Attorney-General should appear to present the scientific evidence and argue the question from the point of view of the public interest. The result was that it could not be established that it was a scientific impossibility that the petitioner could have been the father of the child, and consequently there was no such evidence of misconduct as to justify the Court in granting a decree.

Another instance is furnished by the case of Tickner *v.* Tickner, where the King's Proctor was directed to instruct counsel to argue the nature of the Court's discretion to grant or refuse a divorce.

Appearance by the King's Proctor under the power above mentioned is not the most familiar instance of his function. The 1860 Act made it the rule that decrees of divorce should not be made absolute in the first instance. There is a period, normally six months, between the decision and the moment when it becomes operative. The first or preliminary decree is called the decree *nisi*, this, of course, being the Latin word meaning "unless"; the second or final decree is called the decree absolute, and when that is made, and not until then, the parties are divorced. During the intervening period any member of the public may intervene with a view to proving that the decree *nisi* was obtained by collusion or on the ground that material facts were not brought to the notice of the Court. Anything that has happened during this period may be a material circumstance.

The Act also provides that at any time during the progress of the cause, or before decree absolute, any person may give information to the King's Proctor as to any matter material to the decision of the case, and the King's Proctor may take such steps as the Attorney-General may deem necessary or expedient, and if the King's Proctor shall suspect collusion he may, under the direction of the Attorney-General, and by leave of the Court, intervene in the suit alleging such case of collusion, and he may retain counsel and subpœna witnesses to prove it. A subsequent statute brought nullity suits within the powers of intervention.

It will be noticed at once that where the King's Proctor suspects collusion he must :

(1) Act under the direction of the Attorney-General ; and

(2) Obtain the leave of the Court.

As, however, it is the practice of the King's Proctor to intervene, except in very special cases, only after a decree *nisi* has been pronounced, leave is not necessary, because the King's Proctor has the right, given to everyone, to intervene at that stage without leave.

The usual practice is for the King's Proctor to investigate, and lay before the Attorney-General a case or report which embodies a shorthand note of the hearing, statements of persons who can give evidence, copies of material documents, and a statement of the grounds upon which intervention is suggested. The Attorney-General then considers the whole of the facts and circumstances and gives his direction, either that the King's Proctor should intervene or that he should not.

Once the King's Proctor has intervened, he delivers a pleading, called a plea, in which he sets out the grounds of the intervention and a statement of the facts relied upon in sufficient detail to enable the petitioner to realise what is alleged against him. If the petitioner thinks that the plea does not give sufficient information he may apply to the Court for an order for particulars, so that he may know exactly what case he has to meet. Even if he does not dispute the allegations, the Court must be satisfied. The method adopted in such a case is to give notice of motion, and the Court then decides the

matter upon affidavit. The petitioner who
admits the facts may nevertheless think that he
or she ought to have a divorce on the ground that
the Court should exercise its discretion in his or
her favour. This is treated in the same way as if
the allegations were denied—that is, the petitioner
files an answer and the case is put into the defended list and comes into Court for a hearing
with witnesses on the issues raised. The Court
has full power over costs, and can therefore
order the King's Proctor to pay the costs of an
unsuccessful intervention ; but of course a case
where the allegations are admitted, and the Court
is asked to exercise its discretion, is not an unsuccessful intervention, for then the petitioner has to
excuse what has happened.

The first duty of the King's Proctor is, therefore, to investigate. The work is both difficult
and delicate, demanding the exercise of tact.
He does not, of course, act as a private inquiry
agent playing the rôle of Peeping Tom ; but he
is called upon to examine into unsavoury details
as a result of information given to him by others
who may be influenced by motives neither honourable nor decent. There come before him anonymous letters and offers of information from all
sorts and conditions of people who are concerned

to gratify their spite and malice. But he also receives, though not perhaps so often, communications from persons who act from the highest motives. Sometimes indeed the Judge who has granted a decree on evidence which is adequate thinks that the matter ought to be more closely investigated and sends the papers to the King's Proctor.

Once that official receives information tending to show that a decree has been obtained when it would not have been granted had the real facts been known, he cannot neglect the warning. He does not, however, act merely because he receives information. He examines into the matter in order to ascertain what reliable evidence is available, and then forms his own opinion. Only after the documents and witnesses' statements have been collected and considered is it decided to formulate charges with a view to obtaining the direction of the Attorney-General. Unless intervention is directed, the King's Proctor does not interfere. The Attorney-General, therefore, acts as a kind of Grand Jury upon whom rests the responsibility of saying whether the petitioner shall be subjected to any objection to his decree being made absolute. Much, or perhaps all, of the abuse flung at the King's Proctor ought really to be directed at the

Attorney-General, on whose instructions the King's Proctor is, by statute, bound to act. Once this direction to intervene has been given, counsel is retained to settle the pleadings and advise upon evidence ; and, finally, the intervention cannot in any event succeed unless the Court is satisfied that the case has been made out.

These being the safeguards against unnecessary or vexatious intervention, it is not surprising that no Judge has ever deemed it his duty to censure the King's Proctor. There have, of course, been instances where his intervention has failed. Where allegations are proved by the oral evidence of witnesses, it must happen that a witness is not believed, and therefore that the petitioner succeeds. Such failures are inevitable, and occur in other cases of official work, as for instance when the Public Prosecutor undertakes a prosecution.

One frequent criticism is that the King's Proctor differentiates between the rich and the poor. Nowadays, an official who wishes to distinguish himself is much more likely to be tempted by the limelight of public proceedings against persons of wealth and position than by the favour of individuals obtained by secret favour. The King's

I—14

Proctor has never made any distinction between
any classes of the community, but it is obvious,
even to the casual observer, that his intervention
occurs much more frequently in divorce cases
between parties in a humble walk of life than in
any other, and also that the difference is not to
be accounted for by the fact that such cases are
more numerous than others. The explanation
lies in the circumstance that persons of means
have the advantage of advice from lawyers of the
greatest knowledge and experience and are therefore well informed of the things that will lead to
intervention. They are, therefore, able so to
conduct themselves that objection cannot successfully be made. It may be that sometimes a
party who has means and position has used such
advice to the end that he may conceal the true
facts, but the King's Proctor acts upon evidence,
not upon suspicion. In the absence of reliable
evidence to support an intervention, no objection
will be lodged against a decree. There is also this
consideration : that the life of the poor is more
public than that of any other class. Misconduct
by a person of means may be committed so
privately that it is known only to persons who
have the greatest possible interest in concealing
it. A motor-car, for instance, seldom at the

disposal of the poorer of the poor, may prove a tower of strength to the peccant wealthy. Rarely, if ever, can such means of evasion present themselves in the case of others who have no privacy in any of their doings, and whose conduct is, therefore, likely to be known to many who have no interest in preserving silence, but may even have some motive for speaking out. It is unfortunately the case that collusion may occur, but, for the reasons suggested, the evidence to support the charge is too slight for any chance of a successful intervention.

The usual ground upon which intervention is made is that the petitioner has not brought to the knowledge of the Court circumstances which are material for the Court to know. This ground may cover any of the cases which constitute a bar to a decree, but it is wider. The misconduct of the petitioner since the decree or some gross irregularity in the proceedings may be alleged. It has happened that a petitioner has formed an attachment since the decree *nisi*. Sometimes indeed the petitioner remarries ; more often he or she has considered that the marriage has been dissolved and therefore there is no longer any duty of chastity. It is almost incredible after all these years that persons of ordinary intelligence

should misunderstand the nature of a decree
nisi, but there are such cases, almost invariably
where the offender is poor and always where the
advice of a lawyer has not been obtained.

Upon the King's Proctor bringing the matter
before the Court, the Judge will consider whether
the petitioner has really misunderstood his position, and acted in ignorance, or whether he has
taken the risk of being found out. In any event
it is for the Court to say whether the decree is to
stand, and the party who is in fault cannot ask
the King's Proctor to usurp the function of the
Court.

There are, however, cases where the parties
have come together again. Naturally, in such a
case neither would desire to keep the decree alive.
The proper course to pursue is for the parties
themselves to bring the matter before the Court ;
but reconciliation has sometimes been treated by
simple persons as their own private concern and
they have done nothing. The danger to the
former respondent is that if disputes subsequently
arise the decree may be made absolute ; though
no ground has existed for divorce since the original
offence was condoned. Indeed, in one case it
would appear that the husband's intention was
only to forgive his wife conditionally ; so that if

she displeased him he could fall back upon the decree. The King's Proctor intervenes in such cases in order to have the decree formally rescinded. If the parties have not done that themselves, they have no ground to complain if a public official sees that the records of the Court are kept in proper condition.

There have been far more serious cases of irregularity. Many will remember the case in which Slater's Detectives were exposed. For a long time advertisements had been published broadcast of a kind designed to arouse suspicion in the minds of married people as to the habits of their spouses. The subtlety with which these suggestions, destructive of the mutual confidence which is essential to the happiness of matrimony, were distributed was not equalled by the methods employed. Judges were suspicious, but for a time no definite information could be obtained. At last in one case it was found that the detective employed, despairing of obtaining evidence of the desired misconduct, had made the intended respondent drunk and left him helpless in a house of ill-fame. The consequent exposure of the firm and its methods quickly put an end to its activities, and the profession of private detective received a blow from which it has only been enabled to recover by the exercise of due care, and a proper regard for accuracy and decency. The task of exposing the nefarious system in question was entrusted to the King's Proctor ; and his successful intervention was a salutary lesson to those who think they can deride the law with impunity.

Another class of irregularity which is perhaps due to the ignorant cunning of a few individuals relates to the service of the citation. Great care is taken that the fact of a petition having been presented shall be brought to the knowledge of the respondent, and an affidavit of due service is required before a suit can be set down as undefended. It may not be easy to serve a respondent. During the war, for example, it was often impossible for a petitioner to know where the respondent was to be found. Again, there have been cases where service would certainly have led to a successful defence. There have been one or two cases where the respondent has not been served, but an affidavit of service has been made. This is most unusual, as solicitors do not as a rule omit the precaution of keeping control over the service.

In one case it was discovered that the petitioner and respondent were living together without the respondent having the slightest idea that there had been a petition or that the petitioner had ever contemplated a divorce, for which indeed there were no grounds. The person with whom misconduct was alleged and the respondent had never even heard of one another's existence. The petitioner had, it seems, gone to London on the day of the hearing ostensibly for a day's outing and returned at night resuming ordinary home life.

A more usual form of this trickery was personation. The petitioner or a relative would accompany the clerk who was to effect service, and identify some one as the respondent, wilfully arranging with the personator to be there for that purpose. The subsequent proceedings at the Old Bailey following on the exposure of the conspiracy by the King's Proctor have rendered would-be divorcees somewhat chary of this particular device.

Another form ot concealment, which was speedily found to be likely to result in a conviction, was the giving of a false address by the petitioner. The motive was usually to prevent inquiries at the real address, where it would be almost inevitable that the slightest investigation would disclose the fact that the petitioner was living in adultery. The scheme had obvious and fatal objections, not the least of which was that it rendered inevitable that any inquiry would result in the discovery that the petitioner had committed perjury in swearing that he or she lived at the address given. The Court would thus be informed of an abuse of its procedure coupled with a criminal offence. The trick thus speedily lost its attraction, and is only now played by a few individuals who re-discover both the device and subsequently the unpleasant results of this form of deceiving the Court.

Occasionally it is found that petitioners untruly allege that they are domiciled in this country. The Court exercises jurisdiction to dissolve a marriage, not of residents, but of persons domiciled here. Mere residents who are not domiciled have been known to seek matrimonial relief here. The reason may be financial, for often the cost of taking action in the proper country is too great for their means, but it may also be due to the fact that in some countries divorce is still impossible and, consequently, unless a petition can be presented here the marriage cannot be dissolved. There are not many such cases. Akin to them are the cases which sometimes occur where there has been a divorce abroad. If the parties were properly divorced by a competent Court, then the English Courts will not make a futile decree which has no effect. It may be the King's Proctor's duty to obtain evidence of divorce in any country in the world, so that the Court here may be satisfied that its jurisdiction is being invoked by a person properly entitled to seek relief at its hands.

Most cases of irregularities which may call for the consideration of the King's Proctor can be grouped under the absolute or discretionary bars to a decree. These, I repeat, are :

Connivance, condonation, and collusion where the Court will not grant a decree ; and adultery, unreasonable delay, cruelty, desertion or wilful separation, before the adultery alleged against the respondent, and wilful neglect or misconduct conducing to the alleged adultery, in any of which the Court has a discretion to grant or refuse a decree.

Every petitioner is bound to be honest to the Court, and if he or she fails to disclose any fact which will or may lead the Court to refuse a decree, then intervention will be at his or her cost, and will probably lead to the rescission of the decree.

Connivance and collusion are most difficult to

detect. Indeed, it is not many years since a well-known respondent admitted publicly that his divorce was arranged, and that the misconduct alleged and not disputed by him had never, in fact, occurred. He had waited until the decree had been made absolute before taking the world into his confidence. A man in a humbler sphere of life, who also attempted to bring about a divorce by the same means, was found out by the King's Proctor and ultimately convicted. In certain classes of society it is found that the people who know will not give evidence—those moving in the same circles from a spirit of friendship and those moving in humbler spheres of life being possibly actuated by other motives. Connivance is not likely to be set up by a respondent who is not disputing the divorce. As a rule, therefore, the issue if raised at all is raised by the respondent as a defence. The King's Proctor is not entitled, of course, to intervene on any ground which has been raised and decided at the hearing.

Condonation, however, may often be met with. The nature of condonation is often misunderstood. It is not merely forgiveness. The guilty party must be replaced on the matrimonial footing. It is not essential that sexual intercourse shall be resumed ; but, if it is, then the petitioner would be hard put to it to prove that there had been no condonation. The instance already mentioned of the husband who received back his wife, without having the decree rescinded, affords an example of condonation. The offender, however, is not given licence to continue misconduct, and may therefore forfeit the position thus restored by further misbehaviour.

Discretionary grounds are in relation to the King's Proctor of varying importance. Unreasonable delay in presenting a petition will almost inevitably be obvious on reading the petition. The Judge at the trial will be sure to raise the question, and no prudent solicitor would launch the petition without first satisfying himself that there are at least some considerations in his client's favour which may weigh with the Judge. It may be assumed with some confidence that, if the point is to be raised at all, it will be raised and disposed of before the King's Proctor has seisin of the case.

Cruelty, desertion, wilful separation, wilful neglect, or misconduct seem at first blush to be allegations which a respondent would be sure to raise at the trial. It is found in practice that respondents may take up either of two attitudes. The one is to say in effect : " True, I was guilty

of misconduct, but who are you to complain ?
See what a life you led me, and the straits into
which I fell through your fault." On the other
hand, there are numerous occasions where it is
found that a respondent prefers to allow a petition
to go undefended for the very reason that it dis-
solves a union which has become repugnant to
him or her, even though the charge levied is false.
Such cases may be of great hardship. The petitioner is seeking relief because of the matrimonial
offences alleged against the respondent, but in
the circumstances it is the latter who is entitled
to sympathy. Take the case of a woman who has
suffered the greatest ill-treatment and discourtesy,
but who, until 1923 at least, might easily be in
such a position that divorce is impossible on her
petition. The very thought of being tied to the
man is repugnant to her, and she may not un-
naturally think that the reproach of infidelity to
him is of no importance compared to her freedom.
To enter no defence to a charge of adultery, real or
imaginary, will give her the freedom which alone
she desires. The decree is granted. The King's
Proctor intervenes, and the Court is asked to
decide whether in the circumstances the petitioner,
and not the respondent, is to be allowed a remedy
to which he is not entitled as of right.

Such cases are painful and naturally lead to criticism of a system which inevitably results in such cases in a ruined marriage being kept in existence. The hardship is apparent, but it must be remembered that the duty of the King's Proctor is to see that the Court is properly informed of all the relevant circumstances. It is the petitioner who poses as the injured party : to the petitioner is redress to be given. The respondent does not assert a right to divorce on any of the grounds allowed by the law, and therefore cannot claim the indulgence of the Court. While such a position may be the outcome of the statute law as it is now, the King's Proctor must do his duty. The injustice which results is not one which the King's Proctor or the Attorney-General has the right to redress, and the Court has to consider whether its discretion shall be exercised in favour of the petitioner, not of the respondent.

Happily such cases where the merits can be said to be almost wholly with the legally guilty party are not very numerous. In most cases where such a discretionary bar exists the fault is more evenly balanced, and demands for sympathy are not excessive on either side. Still, the fact remains that, as the law now stands, a decree may be rescinded which a Judge who was entirely unfettered and entitled to come to a decision *ex equo et bono* might decline to disturb. It is a matter for grave consideration whether the discretion may not be enlarged, but this is most conveniently to be considered when the principles upon which the Court acts in exercise of its discretion fall to be discussed.

One of the most usual grounds for intervention is the adultery of the petitioner. A cynical practitioner has declared that no petition is ever lodged before the petitioner has chosen a new spouse. There is sufficient truth underlying the remark to make it pungent, but, like most general observations, it does not reveal the whole truth. The dominant motive is probably a desire for freedom. Nevertheless, it is a curious fact that often it is discovered that, although the respondent has formed a new alliance, he or she is not alone in that, and both parties have abundantly consoled themselves. Why petitioners should attempt to obtain a divorce in such circumstances is not wholly a mystery. There are still a large number of individuals who are not content with an irregular union, but desire the superior status or greater respectability of matrimony. Again, it must be remembered that some people, although they do not themselves mind living an immoral life, have the greatest repugnance to casting the stigma of bastardy upon their children. It is the desire to have a place in society, to have their union sanctioned by law, and to give their children the rights and position due to legitimacy, that seems to influence guilty petitioners to seek relief against partners who are only equally guilty with themselves.

The facts giving rise to the question whether intervention shall take place or not vary almost indefinitely in such cases. The evidence varies from what is mere suspicion on the one hand to overwhelming proof of open and notorious adultery on the other. In considering the weight to be attached to such evidence, the King's Proctor and the Law Officer must bear in mind that, where adultery is alleged on probable evidence, any exercise of discretion is for the Court. At the same time there is a margin between mere suspicion and strong evidence, and in border-line cases care has to be taken to see that petitioners are not vexatiously pursued, but that nevertheless circumstances which demand judicial examination are not passed over.

The fact that the evidence is collected and examined in the first instance by an experienced public official, and then considered coolly and dispassionately by the Law Officer before the attention of the Court is drawn to the case, is the security enacted by Parliament.   It is in such cases as these now under discussion that intervention fails on the rare occasions that the allegations of the King's Proctor have not been held to have been established, and also where, though his intervention is held to have been justified, nevertheless the Court has decided to make the decree absolute.   It is here that there is found opportunity for widely divergent views to be held as to the true inference to be drawn from the facts admitted or proved.

Some cases, however, are beyond doubt.   There was once a divorce petition lodged by a solicitor who was the petitioner's paramour, and the respondent was decoyed into a brothel in another country by the solicitor's agent.   The King's Proctor intervened, and in the ultimate result the solicitor fled the country and was struck off the rolls.   In another case the petitioner, after obtaining a decree and having sworn in her evidence that she had not seen her husband for ten years, was taken from Court by her mother-in-law to a lying-in hospital where she gave birth to a child on the same day.   Another case may be recalled where a lady was found to have had an exceptionally lurid career and was driven to inventing a wicked twin sister whose misdeeds were being attributed to her, who was, in her own estimation, of unspotted reputation. In her case the ultimate result was a term of six months' imprisonment for perjury.

Most of the cases of intervention are based on the disregard of the inflexible rule that the petitioner must reveal his or her own matrimonial misconduct. In many of them, the petitioner admits that the intervention is justified, but seeks to show that nevertheless the circumstances are such that the fault can and should be overlooked. The words of the section are " that the Court shall not be bound to pronounce " the decree. In other words, the Judge has an unfettered discretion.

It used not to be thought so. In a case of Morgan *v*. Morgan, decided in 1869, Lord Penzance mentioned three classes of cases in which he thought discretion might properly be exercised : first, where the respondent induced the petitioner to believe that he or she was dead and the petitioner was thereby led to marry again ; secondly, where a wife was compelled by her husband to lead an immoral life ; and, thirdly, although Lord Penzance indicated that this remained to be

I—15

decided, where the petitioner had committed adultery which had been condoned and after-wards the respondent committed adultery with which the petitioner's former lapse had nothing to do.   Lord Penzance expressly added that there might be other classes, but repudiated the idea that the Court should grant or withhold a divorce upon the mere footing of the petitioner's adultery being, under the whole circumstances of each case, more or less pardonable or capable of excuse. " Upon such materials," he added, " two minds will hardly ever form a judgment alike, and the same mind will often appear to others to form contradictory judgments on what seem to be similar facts. This invites public criticism, and shakes public confidence in the justice of the tribunal."

Whether Lord Penzance's criticism is justified or not, the rule that he rejected has now been established. In 1917 the Court of Appeal had to consider what was the power of the Court under the section. The Judge of First Instance had come to the conclusion that it has " an unfettered discretion, and that it is neither desirable nor possible to lay down definite and rigid rules by which it should be guided in all cases. To do so would be to destroy a discretion the exercise of which must depend upon the particular facts of each case.   At the same time, that discretion must not be exercised in a haphazard fashion, but . . . cautiously and carefully, and as far as possible, consistently, not only in regard to the parties themselves, but also with reference to the interests of public morality."

The Court of Appeal approved the Judge's opinion as to the exercise of his discretion.   In 1919 Sir Henry Duke stated certain circumstances which in his view warranted the exercise of discretion in favour of a petitioner.   These were four :

First, the interests of the children, who ought to have a home with the sanction of decency ;

Secondly, the position of the woman with whom misconduct, alleged by the King's Proctor, was committed ;

Thirdly, the position of the respondent, there being no prospect that refusal of relief would effect a reconciliation ; and

Fourthly, the interest of the petitioner that he should be able to marry and live respectably.

The President added : " This discretion is not to be exercised eagerly or indeed readily, but with some degree of stringency."

In 1922 a decree was granted to a man whose

wife deserted him in 1889 and who began to live
with another woman in 1890, and continued to do
so until her death in 1921.   He heard of the wife's
misconduct in 1894, but took no proceedings for
divorce until 1922, because he thought his own
misconduct was a bar to proceedings.   This case
is probably the high-water mark.   The Judge was
probably influenced by the fact that allowance
must be made for the ignorance and circumstances
of persons in humble life.   The whole of the cases
have recently been reviewed in a case which was
referred to the King's Proctor so that the Court
might have the advantage of a full argument
from counsel.   The President, after consideration,
reaffirmed the principle that the Court had been
given an unfettered discretion.[1]   The petitioner
was actually living with a man who desired to
marry her.   The President did not think that in
the circumstances virtue and morality would be
promoted by a decision which would leave her
under a disability to remarry until she became
a widow, and he accordingly gave a decree.

I have explained that when Parliament made
divorce a remedy available in judicial proceedings
and thus gave to the general public relief which
had hitherto been confined to those who could

[1] Tickner v. Tickner, 1924, 40 T.L.R. 667.

afford the costly remedy of a special Act of Parliament, it was speedily found necessary to devise some special safeguard which had never been found essential in ordinary civil proceedings. The fact that in certain events which were jealously circumscribed the victim of an unfortunate marriage could dissolve the union proved to be an irresistible temptation to those who desired the same freedom but could not or might not be able to show the Court that they were justly entitled to a decree.

The alteration of the grounds for divorce is a matter for Parliament alone, but so long as divorce by consent is not sanctioned by the law of the land, there always will be spouses who ardently desire to dissolve a union which has become intolerable to them, although the law gives them no means of attaining their desire for freedom. There will, therefore, always be a temptation to such persons to obtain by some device or pretence the relief which the law denies them, and, further, many of them will be actively or passively assisted by the other party who equally desires the same relief. Our Courts are not organised to exercise an inquisitional jurisdiction. To entrust, therefore, to the Divorce Court itself the duty of investigating cases where there is reason to suspect that the Court has been or may be imposed upon, is repugnant to all the ideas which underlie the administration of justice in our country. Parliament for this reason adapted an existing office and imposed upon the holder of it, under the direction of the Attorney-General, the duty of bringing to the notice of the Court any case in which there is evidence to support a definite allegation that a decree may have been obtained when the law does not allow it or directs that the Court shall only grant it after due consideration of all the relevant circumstances.

He is responsible to the Court, but the Court is not answerable to him. His function is to receive information and to test it, so that the Court can be reasonably assured that its process is not being made available in cases where the law does not assist the litigant. The King's Proctor is an independent public official, and the success with which he has on the whole fulfilled his functions is shown by the fact that, although intervention may be undertaken by any member of the public, it is the rarest event for anyone else to move the Court in divorce cases. The individual who thinks that a decree should not be made absolute invariably submits his information to the King's Proctor and abides by the result, even in the numerous cases in which no intervention takes place.

Whether there is really any need for the existence of such an official is a question upon which different opinions may well be held. At present, he has no option; for his duties are imposed by statute and, so long as the law stands as at present, he must continue. It may be thought by some that a Judge, who, both at the Bar and on the Bench, has had a wide experience in sifting and weighing evidence, does not really need his assistance in divorce cases; that if a party commits the offence of conspiring to defeat justice or of perjury, then he or she may be left to the risk of criminal proceedings, which may be instituted in the same way as against a similar offender in any ordinary civil action. There is, however, this observation—that in a civil action the judgment so obtained may be set aside, but in divorce proceedings other parties may be involved; for either party may remarry, and it would be unthinkable to set aside a decree which has been acted upon by the remarriage of one of the parties.

Whether the Court has power to rescind a decree even after it has been made absolute may be fit for academic discussion, but no one has ever made the attempt to move the Court, and the practical consequences might render such a course a public calamity. The existing system does aim at the prevention of the mischief feared by Parliament, before it is too late. The action of the King's Proctor is subjected to supervision, and can never be successful without a Judge concurring, for it is the Court and not the King's Proctor who is charged with the duty of saying whether any decree is to be set aside, and, before the decision, every petitioner whose conduct is called in question is given an opportunity of meeting the charge, which must be formulated with precision, and supported by evidence which satisfied the Judge.

Criticism of the King's Proctor usually takes two forms, leaving on one side those which are directed to the existence rather than the methods of that official. The first is that he stirs up a mass of unsavoury details which had better in the public interest be left undisturbed. It cannot be denied that the circumstances which he brings to light must very frequently be most nauseating, and the publicity thus given to them may have harmful results. In all unpleasant cases this problem has to be faced. The King's Proctor is not the only public servant whose actions may be criticised on this ground, and it calls imperatively for the exercise of good sense and good taste. It also often happens, especially in view of the modern trend to exercise judicial discretion more frequently than has been the case, that the King's Proctor is bound to intervene in order to call attention to the petitioner's own lapses from virtue, but in the result the decree is confirmed. The result is that the petitioner suffers exposure and is put to great expense, but no other consequence follows, for the desired relief is granted. As such cases are necessarily cases of hardship, and the petitioner receives the sympathy of the Court, the intervention does then seem unnecessary and cruel. It is difficult to see how this can be avoided while the present system exists. If the King's Proctor were not to intervene in such instances, he would be usurping the jurisdiction of the Court, and an alteration giving him the discretion would add one more province absorbed by the administrative from the judiciary.

It is possible that some alteration in the law might be devised to cover such cases of hardship, but it would be difficult to devise appropriate words which would be restricted to them and them only. Moreover, as they occur in circumstances where the Court has unfettered discretion, the criticism is often based on the fact that A has failed where B, who is just as bad, has been successful. The King's Proctor has not, and must not be allowed to acquire any control over the judiciary, and the divergent decisions of particular Judges cannot be avoided so long as their jurisdiction is discretionary and not confined by definite rules. Whether the discretion should exist and, if it is to exist, whether it should remain unfettered, are questions upon which difference of opinion may well occur, and can only be resolved, if at all, by statute.

The other criticism is that the King's Proctor discriminates against the poor. In the sense that he does so consciously and deliberately, the accusation is ludicrously untrue, but it cannot be denied that the humble classes are more readily detected in wrongdoing than those whose means enable them to obtain good advice and to take precautions to secure secrecy. A person who cannot afford to consult a lawyer as to his position, or, as more frequently happens, does not realise that he ought to seek advice, will make up his own mind, possibly with assistance from others in his own station of life, as to what is permissible. He will often make up his mind wrongly, and thereby be open to intervention. To some extent this is inevitable, but the Judges in cases of discretion will always bear in mind the knowledge of law and procedure that the individual has or can command, and therefore the person of lowly position will be judged more leniently than one who has no excuse. The other class where a man uses his means to cloak his misdeeds and succeeds in his attempt is not open to the same answer. If A, being poor, has deliberately sought to delude the Court and is detected, it is no reason against his being made to suffer that B has been successful because he is wealthy. Such a state of affairs ought not to exist, but the logical conclusion leads rather to the strengthening of the powers of the King's Proctor than to any other conclusion. It is to be regretted that collusion is known to exist, but the instances where it can be proved are few compared with the number that are suspected for probable reasons. On the other hand, to institute an inquisition in order to correct this abuse would be an evil far greater than the one sought to be removed thereby.

On the whole, therefore, it must be conceded that in the present position of the law it is inevitable that the King's Proctor, or some other official, acting under the high authority of the Attorney-General, shall have the duty of assisting to keep the practice of divorce clean and free from abuse. He may inflict hardship in some cases but, as matters stand, he has succeeded in so administering his duties that the criticism legitimate and illegitimate that is levelled against his office is surprisingly small.

VIII

LEAVES FROM A LAWYER'S NOTE-BOOK

Are Our Law Courts Cruel?

SIR HALL CAINE has recently contributed
to the columns of the Press a very interesting
and powerful letter in which he examines the
proceedings which took place lately before a
coroner's court. He dealt also in an arresting
fashion with some much larger questions. It is
my purpose, as one who was for long deeply
interested in the administration of justice, to
examine both the general and the particular
questions which he raises. The general in such
a matter is obviously more important than the
particular. I begin, therefore, by addressing myself to the consideration of the question whether
our Law Courts are in fact unnecessarily cruel and
brutal in their methods of conducting legal
business.

In my opinion, this question must be answered
in the negative. There is certainly no system of
justice in the world in which the interests of

accused persons, and a proper protection for witnesses, are more tenderly and zealously guarded. To deal with the case of prisoners first : The English Criminal Courts are the admiration of the civilised world. The startling contrasts which exist between their methods and those of Latin jurisprudence are too notorious to require emphasis. But it is in fact the case that our law has evolved, and actually acts with inflexibility upon, the noble principle that every accused person is presumed to be innocent until his guilt is demonstrated to the satisfaction of the Court. I must not, of course, be supposed to be dealing with very small matters in very small Courts. I have not, for instance, in my mind the method in which the cases are tried before local magistrates of those who are alleged to have broken rules for the regulation of speed for motor-cars. I do not dismiss these matters as unimportant ; but I shall nevertheless be understood if I say that in all grave matters, and before all serious Courts in this country, there is a deep realisation that this principle lies at the root of the administration of our criminal system.

An illustration may be given which has occasioned some bewilderment and much controversy among laymen, and sometimes even among lawyers. It has, for instance, been discussed whether an advocate, to whom his client has admitted guilt, is nevertheless morally justified in arguing in order to prove his innocence. Of course he is. He must not, indeed, say that he " believes " him to be innocent ; no advocate in any Court would be allowed to say this in any statement ; but he is most properly allowed to " submit " every consideration which the guilty person, if qualified by technical knowledge, might have made for himself. The robust common sense of Dr. Johnson long ago penetrated to the root of the whole matter when he observed : " Sir, the advocate is not to usurp the function of the Judge." It is just because the English law in all circumstances, until complete proof is established, infers the innocence of the accused that this necessary rule was embodied in our judicial system.

It has sometimes been argued that it can no longer apply in a case where the accused person has himself made a confession. This is an absurd and ignorant argument. Has an innocent person never admitted the commission of a crime ? Has hysteria disappeared from the world ? Have persons mentally unbalanced, though not certified as lunatics, been completely removed ? Are there not innumerable cases on record in which men and women have admitted the commission of crime in order to protect a relative, a lover, or a spouse ?

The making of a confession, therefore, never concludes the matter. It is the duty of the advocate to look at the case as a whole, to select from the complex of facts all the considerations which seem to him to operate in favour of the prisoner, and to place these facts as persuasively as he can before the tribunal.

The foregoing observations will have made it plain that in my opinion there is neither cruelty nor inhumanity in the treatment of prisoners in our Courts ; that, on the contrary, they are sheltered and protected to a degree unknown in any other country in the world, except in our own Dominions. I do not examine, within the limits of this article, the state of affairs in the United States of America, for many qualifications and reservations would be required in dealing with so vast a subject.

I proceed to consider the next topic in my examination : Do counsel at the Bar torture witnesses unnecessarily ? Is bullying rife in our Law Courts ? Are witnesses subjected to annoyance, humiliation, and pain by questions not really germane to the immediate issue ?

It is my opinion that in broad perspective none of these mischiefs really exists in our system. It is, of course, true that counsel occasionally exceeds alike his duty and privilege. It is the duty of the Judge to correct this. It would be absurd to say that every counsel and every Judge ideally discharge their respective functions. But in this country nearly all do. The most irregular, the most utterly indefensible, cross-examination which I recall in thirty years was that of Mr. Winston Churchill in a recent libel action. Here I suspect that the very able and experienced Judge tolerated the gross licence of the cross-examination because he had no doubt as to the issue of the matter, and was anxious to run no risk of irritating the jury by appearing too favourable to the plaintiff. But it would, in my opinion, have been more edifying if he had run this risk and disallowed as irrelevant, offensive, and almost unprofessional 70 per cent. of the cross-examination.

Another learned Judge in a case tried a year or two ago amazed me by making the observation : " In this case I shall not exclude *any* evidence." This indication surely betrayed a most astonishing misconception of duty. The wisdom of many generations of learned and sophisticated lawyers

I—16

has equipped us with a law of evidence which is the admiration of the world. Judges ought to admit or exclude evidence, not by reference to the nature of the particular case which engages their attention, but by reference to the binding and intelligible rules which are an indispensable element in the law of the land.

I come now to the task and duty of counsel. It must not be forgotten that in many cases the issues are of such a nature that severe and even very wounding cross-examination is required in the sacred interest of justice itself. The obvious explanation of this necessity is that issues are often raised in Law Courts which are themselves of a severe, wounding, cruel, and even insulting character. It would be very difficult, for instance, to cross-examine a professional blackmailer or a card cheat without running the risk of hurting his feelings. Who, for instance, could have cross-examined Queen Caroline with amenity? Yet justice in such cases could not be elucidated without the most searching, offensive, and exasperating cross-examination. There are, of course, certain recognised limits well known to all experienced counsel, and rightly insisted upon by the extraordinarily able Judges whom we have the good fortune to possess in this country to-day. The broad test of the legitimacy of what I may call, in its classical sense, an " offensive " cross-examination, is whether that which is put to the witness is relevant to the actual, the determining issues raised by the litigation.

Where, of course, the credit of the witness is itself a fact in issue, it is difficult actually to define in words the limits which must be observed in cross-examination. But every counsel who knows his work is instinctively aware of them. He realises that the admirable common sense of a jury will understand, and give due value to, matters elicited by him reflecting upon the reliability of a witness. But he knows also that if he exceeds his legitimate ambit and declines into positive cruelty, he is very likely to induce a sympathetic reaction which would be fatal to his own client. It would, for instance, be patent madness in an advocate to ask a female witness, even though her credit in other than sexual matters was in issue, whether she had had an illegitimate child fifteen years ago.

These general observations may serve as a preface to the few remarks which I should like to make upon the special subject of Sir Hall Caine's letter ; and I would at once make it plain that in the main I think that his criticisms, made with great literary power and feeling, are well founded. The facts to which he calls attention were indeed very simple.

A female child, sixteen years old, was murdered late at night in the streets of London. A day or two later a boy, aged nineteen, gave himself up to the police confessing that he had committed the crime. The matter came for examination before a coroner's inquest. The mother of the murdered child stated that, although living with her at the time of her death, the girl had been brought up by another person whom her husband on his deathbed had asked to undertake the guardianship of her child. In fact (so it would appear) the child was illegitimate, and was born some years after the death of the husband of the witness. Probably Sir Hall Caine is right in his surmise that the mother wished to protect herself from the risk of censure for allowing so young a child to be upon the streets. If the facts, as related by Sir Hall Caine, are correct, I agree with some of his strictures, although not with all, upon the conduct of the matter.

I do not agree that it was unnecessary to press the witness as to the reasons which had led her to make a false statement upon oath. The mere fact that, for a motive so inadequate, she had given false evidence might well incline even a prudent Judge to test the matter further, in case some explanation underlay the incident which it might be material for the jury to learn. The issues, indeed, which require determination by a coroner's jury are quite correctly stated by Sir Hall. But it is a common, and has often proved a useful, practice for such a jury to add riders to their verdicts. All kinds of reasons can be imagined, which I do not suggest existed in the case under discussion, but which might lead a witness to make a material misstatement of fact in such a matter, and which ought to be known to a jury to whom the duty of examining the matter is committed. When once a witness has lied, a special degree of caution is imposed upon the Judge.

But I agree with Sir Hall that when the facts, as related by him, were once ascertained, no public prosecutor who knew his business would have treated the matter as one which warranted a prosecution for perjury. In fact, to talk of such a prosecution (if the coroner did) was simply silly. But it may be pointed out that it is the duty of witnesses to tell the truth; that it is the duty of the most humane Judge to make an unfavourable comment, measuring his severity to the occasion, where witnesses make statements which are untrue; and it may also be pointed out that, if the witness in question had not chosen, in order to protect her supposed interests, to deceive the Court upon oath, it is highly probable that no attention at all would have been drawn to the illegitimacy of her child's birth. And it must also be pointed out that it is, I suppose, one of the inconveniences of having illegitimate children, that if they become either famous, notorious, or tragic, the fact of their illegitimacy, and therefore the frailty of their mother, is almost certain to be discovered.

I agree, however, entirely with Sir Hall, again assuming, as I naturally do, the accuracy of his statement, that the anonymous and silly communication sent to the coroner did not possess the slightest relevance to the inquiry; and should not in any conceivable circumstances have formed part of the evidence put before the jury. Sir Hall Caine is probably aware that the methods of inquiry pursued at coroners' inquests are not identical with those adopted in the ordinary Courts of Law. There is much to be said in favour of the view that the methods adopted in such Courts are very often both lax and loose. I have not, I confess, often had my attention

directed to a greater irrelevance than the admission
(if made) of such a document as part of the matter
proper to be laid before a jury.

I greatly admire the humanity which enlisted
the eloquent pen of Sir Hall Caine in the support
of this case. I have frankly admitted the justice
of any criticism of his which seemed to me to be
well founded. He believes (I suspect), as I
earnestly believe, that justice is more mercifully,
and more dispassionately, administered in this
country than in any other in the world. I welcome the opportunity of making these observations
upon a branch of our administration in which I
spent thirty years of my life.

 . . . . .

Judge and Jury

In a *cause célèbre* tried not long ago the jury
had apparently arrived at a conclusion very
favourable to the plaintiff. The Judge appeared
much less favourably disposed. The matter was
finally dealt with after a series of somewhat complicated, and perhaps even technical, questions
had been submitted by the Judge to the jury.
The jury gave certain answers to those questions,
and thereupon the Judge on many of the more

important issues of the case, founding himself upon considerations of law, gave judgment in favour of the defendant. This development was certainly unexpected by the public, and has given rise to very considerable controversy. It is therefore worth while to make plain to the general public what respectively are the functions of the Judge and of the jury.

The general principle may be laid down quite plainly, and was made plain in the famous case of R. *v.* The Dean of St. Asaph : Judges are responsible for matters of law : jurymen are responsible for matters of fact. This doctrine admits of certain qualifications, which do not, however, affect the subject of my present inquiry. But I may give an illustration. Where a question arises in any litigation as to the admissibility of evidence, the facts upon which its admissibility depends are determined by the Judge and not by the jury. This is not entirely logical, but it is a convenient rule. Still, the admission of this rule must not blind us to what is plain law : that all questions of mere fact arising at the trial are for the jury, and for the jury alone. The Judge is perfectly entitled to make plain to the jury the way in which his own mind is working. The Judge, in other words, is perfectly entitled to attempt to impress upon the jury the view which he has himself formed of the facts of the case.

The skill of Judges at *Nisi Prius* may very often be measured by the tact with which they manage their juries. If a Judge has formed a strong view upon the facts of the case, he naturally desires that it shall prevail. And the stronger the Judge the more concerned he is that his view shall be reflected in the conclusion. It has long been recorded of a famous Judge whose tact and knowledge of the world were more conspicuous than his abstract understanding of the science of jurisprudence that he was in the habit of saying, if he tried a case in the winter, " I fear that the jury are in a draught " ; and, if he tried a case in the summer, of saying, " Usher, I think that the sun is in the eyes of the foreman."

It very often happens that the case disclosed by the plaintiff, while, in fact, affording material upon which a sympathetic jury could decide in his favour, is vitiated by some legal fault which cannot be cured. If the matter is plain, it is, in my opinion, the duty of the Judge to take the responsibility of saying : " Whatever view the jury may take of the facts, in law the plaintiff will not succeed, and therefore I will not even allow this issue to go to the jury. If I am wrong, the matter can be taken to the Court of Appeal and I can be put right." But in practice Judges are, not unreasonably, affected by the consideration that, if they do so stop the case, and their view of the law ultimately proves to be incorrect, the matter will be sent back to be re-tried in the Court of First Instance, and all the costs will be thrown away. And so it happens that many Judges, who, if they followed their own instincts as to what the law really is, would stop a case at the end of the plaintiff's case with the abrupt decision that there was no issue of fact that could properly be submitted to the jury, abstain from taking this course from the laudable desire not to add to the cost of the litigation.

The duty of a Judge at *Nisi Prius* has never been more clearly stated than in the case of Ryder *v*. Wombwell: "There is in every case in which such issues arise a preliminary question, which is one of law, viz. whether there is any evidence on which the jury could properly find the question for the party on whom the onus of proof lies. If there is not, the Judge ought to withdraw the question from the jury, and direct a non-suit if the onus is on the plaintiff, or direct a verdict for the plaintiff if the onus is on the defendant."

That great lawyer, Lord Cairns, generalised, as his great legal intellect qualified him to do, the rules which determined for all time the separation of function between Judge and jury. He was dealing with an action of negligence, but he laid down in this limited matter, as was his habit, a general and a permanent principle. " The Judge has to say whether any facts have been established by evidence from which negligence may be reasonably inferred. The jurors have to say whether from those facts, when submitted to them, negligence ought to be inferred. It is, in my opinion, of the greatest importance that the separate functions should be maintained, and maintained distinct. It would be a serious inroad on the province of the jury if, in a case where there are facts from which negligence might reasonably be inferred, the Judge were to withdraw the case from the jury upon the ground that, in his opinion, negligence ought not to be inferred, and it would be, on the other hand, placing in hands of the jurors a power which might be exercised in the most arbitrary manner, if they were at liberty to hold that negligence might be inferred from any state of facts whatever."

The issue to which I am devoting my attention —namely, the separation of the functions of

Judges and jury—was in one most important matter brought to a conclusion by Fox's Libel Act (32 Geo. III, c. 60). This highly important statute put prosecutions for libels on the same footing as other criminal cases. But it established the freedom of the Press in England. The common law had clearly defined the relative provinces of Judge and jury in all proceedings for libel. It was for the Judge to direct the jury what in law a libel is. And then it was for the jury to decide conformably with that direction " whether the particular publication before them was or was not a libel." This was the rule originally, alike in civil and in criminal cases. But Lord Mansfield, the great Chief Justice, to the permanent injury of his illustrious reputation, laid it down over and over again that in a criminal case the only questions for the jury to decide were the fact of publication and the meaning of the words ; and that whether the words were libellous or not was a question of law for the Court to decide. The Chief Justice attempted no inroad upon the rule for civil cases. It may be and no doubt is the fact that the majority of contemporary judges shared this view, but from Mansfield somehow one expected a view more enlightened and fully sustainable.

In 1793 Mr. Fox brought in a Bill to remedy

this abuse, and restore the former practice. Mr. Pitt supported him, and the measure passed. It " declares and enacts " that in all criminal proceedings for libel where the defendant has pleaded not guilty, the jurors may give a general verdict on the whole matter, and shall not be required to find the defendant guilty merely on proof of publication, and of the meaning ascribed to the words in the indictment or information (section 1), or the jury may in their discretion find a special verdict as in other criminal cases (section 3). It is still the duty of the Judge to direct the jury on all questions of law as in all criminal cases (section 2), and he may, if he think fit, state his opinion of the document before him. But the question libel or no libel, in civil and criminal cases alike, must ultimately be decided by the jury, who are thus constituted " the true guardians of the liberty of the Press."

I have, I hope, said enough to make it plain in general to the layman what are the functions of the Judge, and what are the functions of the jury. I cannot presume to give advice to the distinguished men who to-day are administrating justice at *Nisi Prius* : though I would make plain my opinion that the Bench has never been more strongly manned than it is to-day.

But I may, without offence to anyone, indicate the lines upon which I should myself proceed if I were trying a case at *Nisi Prius* to-morrow. If I had formed a clear view upon the facts, reaching the conclusion that justice required a certain decision, I should as tactfully and persuasively as I could insinuate my views into the minds of the jury while contriving to avoid the criticism that I was overbearing them in what was their function and not mine. But I should nevertheless loyally recognise the reality of their function and the separation between it and mine. And such a loyal recognition would make it very necessary that I should not attempt to confuse them. If, therefore, I thought it proper to put a long series of questions to them, I should rigidly confine those questions to fair and intelligible issues of fact of which they, and they alone, are the masters. I use the word "intelligible," because a Judge should be especially careful not to abuse the immense qualities of an average jury by confusing them with questions so complicated that they are unable to disentangle the subtlety of the questions from the facts of which they are the supreme judges. A Judge, in my opinion, if he finds it necessary to address a series of questions to the jury, should so formulate those questions that an average juryman could appreciate them, and thereby remain possessed of his undoubted constitutional claim to be the only judge of the facts.

The traditions of English jurisprudence, the methods on which we conduct our criminal trials, are the admiration of the world. They have been imitated very completely in our self-governing Dominions. Their admirable methods have been largely, if not completely, reproduced in the United States of America. They depend upon the broad and simple principle that what twelve ordinary men (and I suppose I must add ordinary women) think of the facts is, on the whole, more likely to be right than a very highly instructed legal functionary. I believe this view to be well founded.

I suppose I was employed in litigation for nearly twenty years, and very largely in jury cases. I cannot remember, in the thousands of cases which I suppose I must have argued before juries, more than three in which I was absolutely certain that the juries were completely wrong. And even in these three the value of my judgment is diminished by the fact that I was an advocate. But the fact that I found only three may perhaps be accepted as showing that

even where I was an advocate I was not unsuccessful in maintaining a spirit of critical fair-
mindedness. The liberties of England require
in the ultimate resort to be construed, not by
technical persons, very highly instructed, but by
ordinary men—where the issues are those of fact
—who lead ordinary lives and think the ordinary
thoughts of ordinary people. This conclusion
is profound ; because upon it depend the liberties
of Englishmen, the freedom of our institutions,
and the correlation of law with popular opinion.

. . . .

Murder and Confession

There is something in the very word " murder "
which brings a thrill to almost every mind. It is
perhaps a little strange that this dreadful atmosphere should have survived a world-flung tragedy
in which so many millions upon one side were
employed, and rewarded, for the purpose of killing so many millions upon the other. A distinction which, though intelligible, seems, on the
whole, a little strange, has nevertheless survived
between what I may perhaps call public and
private killing. I should have expected that
the valuation of human life would have declined
so much—when one recalls the millions who

perished—that it would have been impossible
to assign quite the same interest to an individual
tragedy. And yet this has not proved to be true.
The case of Vacquier excited after the War as
much attention as it would have done in the year
1913. The charge of which Greenwood was
acquitted gave rise to controversy everywhere
in these islands. For three weeks almost everyone speculated as to the relative guilt of Mrs.
Thompson and Bywaters in a strange tragedy.
The real, and rather surprising, truth is that,
however mortal a toll is taken of human life in
a public quarrel, this is, on the whole, assumed
to be natural; whereas an arresting and un-
diminished interest survives in a matter of
individual drama.

I suppose that when a husband, having quarrelled with his wife, is accused of poisoning her,
wives all over the country who have quarrelled
with their husbands are interested in such a
case, even though the casualty list at the first
or second battle of Ypres may have left them,
had they no men-folk at hazard, comparatively
unmoved. Dramas, in fact, interest the public
in proportion to the probability that it may itself
become involved in such happenings. Public
tragedy, though widely diffused, is easily for-

I—17

gotten, for it often makes no special or individual appeal. But the murder of an individual has always excited an immense, if a morbid and pathological, attention, simply because all people who find themselves in situations at all comparable to those of the principal actors in the tragedy are conscious of a personal interest which might conceivably in its development become extremely vital.

To take human life in a private quarrel is a poignant and terrible thing. Our jurisprudence has bracketed this offence with high treason as the gravest of crimes. And obviously there can be none graver. In a public quarrel men take lives, because they obey orders. The responsibility is not theirs; for they may be shot if they do not obey those orders. A belief that what they do is done for their country justifies violence and even dignifies homicide.

But in a private vendetta the matter is wholly different. Human life is precious to almost everyone who breathes the sweet air of this incomparable world. I have never in my life met anyone who really wanted to die. Even very old people seem to live in an atmosphere of easy hope which to those who are younger contains something altogether pathetic. How many

people has the reader met who wanted to die?
I am not, of course, considering for the purpose
of this question those who live on terms of cruel
and perpetual pain ; for it is obvious that all such,
if they are persuaded that their mischief is incurable, must rather take their chance of oblivion,
of reward, or even of punition in another world
than be content to suffer intolerably in this. I
am dealing with normal people who, on the
hypothesis, must be supposed on balance not to
be very unhappy. These have, according to their
ages, their prospects of life. The insurance
companies will provide them with a scientific
and actuarial estimate of this prospect. The
ordinary individual concerned will probably not
trouble too closely about the insurance office
view. But nearly all of them dearly value life
because it is life and not death. With all its
struggles, all its responsibilities, all its anxieties,
life is worth living for its own sake ; it is worth
living out to its last moment ; it is worth struggling
for to its last expiring agony ; even to the death-
rattle—

> When unto dying eyes
> The casement slowly grows a glimmering square.

And so to destroy life in a private quarrel, and
for an individual motive, is a terrible and pro-

foundly anti-social act. It is unquestionably
just that he who extinguishes life in such a quarrel
should himself be destroyed if the crime be
brought home to him.

I suppose that there is no more poignant or
branded name in the English language than that
of " murderer." Cain was the traditional first
of this red family ; he has had many a bloody
and conscienceless successor. The sombre and
ornate genius of Lytton flung round the figure of
Eugene Aram this awful atmosphere. Murder
has always alarmed humanity, and its morbid
interest has, through the generations, continued
to excite men almost more vividly than public
misfortunes, however terrifying. If you take the
community—men and women alike—and exclude
the tragedies of those closely related to the
victims, a single murder case has, as I have pointed
out, often interested the world more than the
issue of a great battle or even the implications
of a mighty campaign.

I am of opinion that the common judgment
of common people, sustained by the assent of
generations of civilised thought, has wisely
reached the conclusion that the gravest offence
of all is to take human life. And yet the matter
requires a little analysis. For in such a conclusion

we must be careful to avoid the slightest tinge of hypocrisy. I especially exclude myself from the idea that I am in any case suggesting that it can ever be justifiable in a private quarrel to destroy human life. No such right, whatever the provocation may be, can be conceded to individual assertion. Only society organised either for the purpose of war, or for justiciary objects, can dare to make so awful a claim. But it would be interesting to analyse and to determine the relative degrees of obliquity which may attach to the unauthorised taking of human life. Here I have only space for a single illustration. Let me invite an honest expression of opinion upon such a matter. Suppose that a blackmailer had surprised a deep and intimate secret of your life, the publication of which meant ruin to you. Suppose further that he made claims upon you which you could not meet ; and, with the filthy object of blackmailing gain, threatened by exposure to destroy you and everyone you cared for in the world. Suppose again, to make the matter vivid and interesting, that you were walking with him, at the time he made these threats, near a cliff over which it would be quite easy by a simple push to propel him (as, for instance, over the Clovelly Heights) into the sea below. To do so would be obviously wrong, plainly a terrible crime; but how far would it be a crime unforgivable in this world or the next? And which would be the greater crime, that of the man who, in the circumstances supposed, had threatened blackmail, or that of the man who, in the event supposed, had repelled blackmail by the only course, however criminal and life-destroying, which seemed to make its repetition impossible?

Here, with a general, though not, perhaps, a very logical, association, I approach the subject of those cases in which murderers, before the dreadful moment of execution, make confessions of their crime. I naturally do not, in these speculations, encroach upon the field in which my distinguished colleague, the Home Secretary, is supreme. But many questions of great psychological interest, not affecting his department, present themselves for examination in this argument.

It is difficult for an ordinary man to place himself in the position of a condemned and guilty murderer. To do so requires no ordinary imaginative quality. Would one, on the whole, in such an event make a confession or not? Such a man could hardly be foolish enough to suppose, having been guilty of an act so violent and so bloody, that a confession made at the last moment in the hope (surely very paltry) of alleviating divine resentment would procure any serious reconsideration of his penal liability either in this world or in the next. And if you once formed that view there is no particular reason why you should make any confession, because, after all, your family and many of your friends may have continued to believe in you; and it can hardly be an attractive prospect that your wife, your sons, and your daughters should know that you died not only a condemned but an admitted murderer.

I do not, of course, know with exactitude how the mind of a man in this condition would function. One can only conjecture. But if he were a clever man, however perverse, I should suspect that he would reason with himself somewhat in the following way. He would say: " I have done a vile and unforgivable thing. If the accepted basis of religion be sound, there is no forgiveness for me now. A death-bed repentance cannot avail me. How can any heavenly tribunal welcome me, even with a confession on my lips? I did an evil thing in destroying life; for this I must pay the penalty in this world and, if there be one, in the next. If I make no admission, I may at least enable those who come after me to say : ' After all, the man may have been innocent.' If I make a confession, I leave my family in the last stage of humiliation and abasement. To make it can neither help me, nor them, on the road which I now travel." I do not examine the point of view on the other side (although it is strong) of a man who says : " Wicked as I have been, I will not dare to face my Maker with a lie on my lips." Still less do I examine the point of view of him who says : " In the infinite scheme of the Universe we are all ants. I have killed an ant. Who cares ? " I have not discussed, and shall not, for an evident reason, discuss, the very interesting question whether or not, where murderers make confessions, such confessions should be made public. The matter is indeed one of great difficulty ; and its conclusion concerns a department of which I am not the head. But certain elements would seem to emerge with clearness and without controversy. It is, for instance, evident that, if a murderer confesses his guilt and makes it a condition that his confession shall not be made public, such a condition must be observed, for he may make such a conditional confession on grounds entirely creditable to himself, and very convenient to authority. He may desire, for instance, that the Home Secretary shall be relieved from the anxiety of speculating whether or not he has rightly sanctioned such an execution. But he may equally, as I have shown, desire that his son shall not know that his father died as a self-confessed murderer. These problems are for the Home Office; and I realise with how much care and humanity they are reviewed. No relevant issue really arises in the case of a man who has made a confession but has himself protested against its publication. More difficult problems require attention in the case of a man who makes a confession without any reservation, so that the inference may on the whole not unfairly be drawn that he is willing, and perhaps expecting, that that confession should be made public.

But here I touch upon matters of deep argumentative interest; which, I repeat, have exercised the very experienced and able men who discharge, in such matters, the responsibilities of the Home Office. I attempt neither to criticise their conclusions, nor even to examine the problems to which they devote so much experience and so much patience. I merely wish to make it plain that they are confronted in this particular matter with a decision of great poignancy and of great complexity.

. . . . . .

Modern Morals

Several recently reported cases have received wide publicity through the medium of our English Law Courts. They have presented many unedifying features, and may appear to justify inferences very unfavourable to our standard of morals. It is extremely important to draw true and not false inferences from social scandals which are widely advertised. It is not less difficult than it is important.

In the first case which I have in my mind, an Indian Prince fell into the hands of a gang of rogues and blackmailers. His victimisation at the hands of this precious crew, advertised in verbatim reports by our Press, has done grave injustice to the traditional standards by which we receive distinguished Indian Princes in this country, and has added, in no inconsiderable degree, to the welter of public scandal in which we seem recently to have passed our lives.

It is not my object here, for obvious reasons, to discuss the Mr. " A " case in detail; but I will at least say this, that the criticisms made in

the Court of Appeal on the attempt to keep
Mr. "A" anonymous were based neither upon
knowledge, nor upon imagination, nor even upon
common sense. There appeared and there was
a great prospect that the matter might at some
time or other be settled. No one could tell
whether it would be settled before the case, with
all its potentiality for mischief, was opened. It
appeared even to experienced observers more
likely than not that it would be settled before
all its humiliating details were revealed. Counsel
upon both sides were agreed in the desire to
avoid publicity in this particular respect. In
these circumstances it was evidently a high
matter of public policy that an Indian Prince
likely to inherit great dynastic and therefore
Imperial responsibilities should be protected, if
it was in any way possible, from the scandal of
a public and humiliating infamy. The result of
the disclosure has been grave ; nor is it possible
to assign limits to it. It is perfectly true that
when once it became plain that the issue had to
be fought out, the principal character in it could
not remain anonymous, but those who, until it
was plain, attempted to protect the name of an
unfortunate and deserving, if indiscreet, young
Prince from scandalous notoriety, were un-

doubtedly right in the efforts (concurred in by the Judge) which they made. It would of course be ludicrous to draw any inference at all in relation to the morality of English life from the revelations of this extraordinary case. The Indian Prince fell into the hands of a very vulgar, a very ingenious and a very hungry band of rogues. Those who plundered him had as little to do with any English Society, and were as little able to illustrate its weaknesses or morals, as the Loeb child had to do with, or was able to illustrate, the mentality of the children of Chicago.

Another case almost as well advertised recently occupied our Press for a fortnight, almost to the exclusion of every other topic. I refer to the notorious Dennistoun case. Day after day, evening after evening, we were indulged with nauseating adequacy by verbatim reports of a singularly ignoble case. Here again there is a tendency to draw inferences which seem to me altogether unwarranted in order to disparage contemporary morality. The amour of a distinguished soldier is disclosed after his death with melodramatic and very interested hysteria. The David of the piece does not place the husband of the woman whom he loves in the thickest of the battle: he places him (so it is claimed) at headquarters ; or at Gibraltar ; or somewhere else where combatant perils of the war are not menacing. I have no intention whatever of entering upon the details of the Dennistoun case, still less of examining its merits. But while I fully realise that the learned Judge who tried the case was quite entitled to require from the jury such determinations of fact as might enable him to apply the principles of law which were proper to regulate those facts, I greatly regret that he did not find himself able to submit to them a series of questions upon fact which an average jury could have readily understood and answered. I myself read the highly technical and sophisticated questions which the learned Judge submitted to the jury with some degree of bewilderment, though I am not without training in the law. I cannot conceive of any series of questions which a Judge, for his enlightenment, need ask a jury, dealing as they must with issues of fact, which an average common-sense Englishman, who has listened with attention to the case, could not answer without confusion. The questions of Mr. Justice McCardie did not seem to me to fall within this legitimate class. We passed through great judicial and constitutional crises before we succeeded in determining that the facts are in

all cases for the jury, and the law in all cases
for the Judge. If our juries are to be required
to answer a long list of interrogatories, they
ought so to be drawn as to enable the ordinary
man, with precision and without ambiguity, to
appreciate the simple issue of fact upon which
he is asked to pronounce.

But a far broader social question requires
consideration. Are the Mr. " A " case and
the Dennistoun case really illustrative of our
morals to-day? Is English society immoral?
Or is it, to make the matter internationally comparative, rather than personal to ourselves,
more immoral than the society of other great
countries?

The question which is proposed invites very
deep consideration, and may perhaps receive
illustration from some general observations. The
temptations and the passions of the world do not
alter from generation to generation nor from
century to century. Men are men and women
are women. There are still among us Helens of
Troy, and Phrynes, and Cleopatras, and Ninons
de L'Enclos, and equally you may find your
Paris, your Don Juan, your Casanova, and your
De Grammont.

It is no doubt true that, in rude and primitive

stages of civilisation, the necessities of daily labour
hardly lend themselves to light sexual conceptions. We are given to understand, and it may
be true, that the early days of mighty Rome
presented an admirable example of simplicity
and of conjugal chastity. But even here the
story of Lucrece reminds us that high princes were
the slaves of lawless and tempestuous passions ;
and, as Rome became luxurious and extremely
sophisticated, we realise in the love-poems of
Ovid, in the satires of Juvenal, in those of Martial,
and in the story of Petronius, that you have only
to wait long enough in the history of any nation
which wins its way to wealth and luxury to discover a period comparable with that of King
Charles the Second of England. The truth is that
there will always exist on a luxurious society an
entirely immoral fringe, lending colour, in a
degree wholly out of proportion to its numbers,
to a general charge of national degeneracy.
Irregularity of morals is by no means confined to
the governing classes. Our Poor Persons Divorce
provisions make this abundantly plain ; but the
amours of our artisan population, though very
freely reflected in the records of the Divorce
Court, excited little interest and less attention.
In fact the *Daily Herald* seldom referred to

them. The case was different where those who
played conspicuous rôles on the erotic stage
were notorious for either social or public reasons.
Such persons in their difficulties, however much
they might dislike it, commanded five columns a
day from a sympathetic and commercial Press,
before the 1926 Act so severely restricted reports
of divorce cases.

These observations are intended to make it
plain that, in my opinion, a grave injustice is
done to the reputation of English morals by the
extraordinary publicity which we have thought it
proper to allow to cases of this notorious class.
The English attitude has always been slightly
arrogant : " You may know all that there is to
know about us ; then strike your own balance : we
shall not on the whole be losers." And English
life is not unsound at the core. It is certainly, for
instance, not less sound than French life, though
I draw with decision a distinction between the
cosmopolitan outlook and morals of Paris, and
those which, in provincial France, have won so
much admiration. There is, of course, in London, just as there is in Paris, in New York, and
in Berlin, a class in which relaxed conceptions of
moral conduct are condoned, and even admired.
I am unaware of any great and populous capital

in any country, at any stage of the world's history, against which this charge could not have been truly made. The morality of violet Athens in its intellectual prime would have made a monkey blush. In illustration of the morals of Imperial Rome, I have already cited Ovid, Martial, Juvenal and Petronius. The history of the immemorial East requires no illustration beyond that of a faithful rendering of the Arabian Nights. And the Old Testament is occasionally quite frank.

We are, in fact, neither worse nor better than our neighbours. In this connection I attempt a slight comparison, but I hope with reserve, between ourselves and the United States of America. They equally with ourselves have their centres of luxury, indulgence, and enjoyment. I should be very much surprised if it could be established that the moral standards accepted there differ very considerably from those which pass muster among ourselves. I have, for instance, noted with interest that a discussion as to the morality of the stage in New York has been coincident with a similar controversy amongst ourselves. It has quite recently been alleged (I know not with what truth) that the modern stage in New York to-day is tainted by indecency. It is even

alleged that the theatres in New York have little
to learn (and this is high praise) from those of
Paris. It is rumoured that one of those moral
crusades which from time to time is undertaken
in the great Republic has bound itself to stamp
out impropriety in the theatres of New York.
Almost at the same moment a critical movement
is initiated in this country, which has as its object
to demonstrate that 80 per cent. of the plays
produced in London are concerned with morbid
and unwholesome sexual problems. I have not
been to a theatre either in New York or in England
for, I suppose, a period of fifteen years. My
individual opinion upon the issues proposed would,
therefore, possess little value. But even if I
were prepared to assume that the stage in New
York and the stage in London were equally
immoral, these conclusions would not influence
me in the general view which I form of the
morality of the general body of citizens either of
Great Britain or of the United States of America.
Dryden was an extremely immoral playwright.
Dryden's England, outside London, certainly
was not immoral.

In order to ascertain the moral standard of a
country it would never occur to me to do so
stupid a thing as to go to the capital of that

country, for it will always be the clearing-house of indulgence, luxury, and wealth. I would rather, if I were dealing with England, go to the provincial centres of population and to its agricultural community. I would, if I were attempting to reach a clear conclusion upon the morals of the United States of America, avoid its great centres of population and go for guidance to those who, in great waste spaces, are building up and sustaining the character of its people, making all the time their own contribution to that moral average by which and by which alone you must judge a mighty Republic.

And to those who would still draw comparisons between what I may perhaps call the sophisticated element in the United States of America and that of this country, I would remind them that some allowance must be made for the differences in the divorce laws of the two countries. Our own divorce law is, in my opinion, barbarous and prehistoric, but we have at present to live under it. We may succeed one day in altering it; but the road is long and difficult and beset by prejudice. Until we so alter it, it is generally true to say that neither husband nor wife in England can procure release except upon proof of infidelity on the part of his or her spouse.

Very few women, unless they are defenceless in such a case, or extremely anxious to make a change, are prepared to make a public admission of incontinence. Many men are prevented by public or by business positions from making such an admission in their own case. And so it happens that in England unions are stereotyped, and homes nominally preserved, from which happiness has in despair fled. Such a message must, from the very nature of the case, breed immorality. In the United States of America these matters are adjusted more easily, less publicly, and less scandalously. It is no doubt true that in several States the rules of divorce are almost as unaccommodating as with us ; but even here the matter is not desperate, for, unless I am misinformed, a domicile can be procured in a less difficult State which will resolve the conjugal problems of a severer domicile. If, after all, a man and a woman who no longer love one another can obtain release without private or public scandal, they have less excuse for entering upon loose relations with those to whom they could, without great inconvenience, become married. I do not know enough of the social conditions existing in the United States to say whether facility for divorce has, on the whole, proved a good thing or a bad thing. I have always hoped that some American student of sociology would one day give us a monumental book, which would contain more data than have ever hitherto been forthcoming, to tell us whether in a broad perspective the facility for divorce which exists beyond the seas has added to the happiness and well-being of the community. No foreigner could dare to offer an opinion upon a point so difficult and obscure. For in such a connection we have to consider not only the question of the husband and the wife; we have equally to examine the case of the children. Has the American divorce system adequately protected the children of the first marriage? Do social difficulties in this matter present themselves? Has the position of the woman herself been weakened by the fact that, after she has given the best years of her life to her husband, it is possible for him, without extraordinary difficulty, to extrude her from his life, and to marry someone younger? These and similar questions could only be answered by American authorities. Some American writer of standing and knowledge may have already dealt with this question; but, if he has done so, I am not acquainted with his work, although I would very gladly be referred to it.

I am sure of this, that those in America who are inclined to become critical of our morals in England ought to remember that the matrimonial tie in this country is far more difficult to unloose than in the United States of America. It has become easier than it was ; but ecclesiastical influence, illogically exerted, has prevented a logical solution of our own divorce problems ; and by doing so has, in my judgment, immensely contributed both to the chicanery of our Divorce Court proceedings, and to the immorality of certain sections among our people.

The foregoing observations must not be construed as meaning that I dispute the fact that there has, since 1914, been a decline, disturbing but not alarming, in the standard of public morals. I think that there has. But you cannot suddenly call upon twenty million of the youth of the world to kill one another without producing certain rather ugly psychological consequences. Many are killed ; those who survive have undergone bitter experiences. The mental changes produced in man by a war waged with the intensity of the Great War finds its reactions upon women ; for anything that profoundly influences, and even transforms, one sex, for however limited a period, is certain to be reflected, even in quite a different sphere of emotion, among the opposite sex. For the sexes, physically, morally, and mentally, are interdependent.

The war produced a spirit of fine reckless-ness among the actual combatants. We rightly acclaim and reward this spirit ; for it was indeed indispensable to the victory which we won. But recklessness is not a quality which you can segregate in a water-tight compartment. Once admitted in a man's nature, perhaps to become his master, it will begin to dominate quite differ-ent and unrelated sides of his character and temperament. And so there has quickly suc-ceeded to the actual strife a great increase in violence and crime ; and an undoubted relaxation of the standards of sexual and indeed of all moral conduct. A familiar illustration is to be found in what were known as " war marriages." A young man, surrounded by desperate dangers in the trenches, which after ten days' leave he knows that he must again undergo, returns to London. He is determined, and small blame to him, that these days at least shall be days—and the nights that follow nights—of pleasure. Per-haps at some night club he meets an attractive young member of the " war-woman " class. The attraction, if fugitive, is warm and mutual ; there arises quickly in the minds of both the question : " Why should we not marry ? " They often did. In case of the worst, from the young wife's point of view, there was after all the pension ; and for both there was at least a week of undiluted, if hectic, pleasure. It would be ludicrous to expect that many of such unions could have permanently endured upon terms of sustained happiness, and so we find the Divorce Court, for years after the Armistice, paralysed by an unprecedented congestion of divorce cases, about 70 per cent. of which were the result of the War.

A further consideration, by no means to be left out of account in the kind of social analysis which we are superficially attempting, is to be found in the imitative faculty of human beings. Crippen killed Belle Elmore ; having killed her, he found himself embarrassed by the existence on the premises of a substantial corpse, which it was extremely difficult to dispose of conveniently and with discretion. He therefore attempted the horrible task of cutting her into small bits, for the purpose, so to speak, of reticent and piecemeal distribution. After Crippen, Patrick Mahon and the cold-blooded bungalow murder. Who could doubt that Mahon owed something to the inspiration—if in such a connection I may be allowed the term—of Crippen? And then again, although one would have thought that the previous examples were not altogether encouraging, we find quite a young man, Norman Thorne, engaged in a detestable murder and attempting to dispose of his victim in the same gruesome and difficult manner. The psychology of crime has not within twelve years received more bizarre and terrible illustration than in the fateful period through which we have lived since the outbreak of the Great War. Take, for instance, a case to which I have already referred, the Loeb murder in Chicago. I have had occasion in the course of my life to make a somewhat careful study of medical criminology. I am hardly aware of a case in the history of crime which has illustrated more vividly the pathological degeneracy to which the minds of young children may yield surrender.

I do not intend here, although I have views upon the subject, to discuss how far this orgy of post-war crime is itself to be affiliated upon the passions excited by the war; but the subject certainly deserves fuller consideration than it has hitherto received.

Still another tentative observation may be risked. The United States themselves do not appear, in the eyes of cautious and friendly observers in other countries, to have entirely escaped the changes which the last decade has brought. The number of violent crimes, disquieting even ten years ago, has undergone a sinister increase. The war spirit—short-lived as was the actual period of co-operation—did not fail during, and after, that period to produce reckless reactions comparable with those which I have analysed in Europe. Perhaps, too, there is another explanation, more formidable because more widely flung, and probably destined to last longer. May it not be the fact that the attempt to force Prohibition upon a nation not yet ready for it, naturally independent and self-reliant, never formally consulted, may, by the denial of respect to a particular law, have impaired ultimately the respect due to the whole law? For it must never be forgotten that law in a civilised country is one majestic whole. You cannot without risk to that venerable fabric enable citizens to pick and choose ; to say, " Here is a law which I respect ; I will obey it," and of another law, " This is ridiculous and unfair ; I do not hold it binding upon my conscience ; and I propose to violate it." I saw many signs on my last visit to the United States that an almost general dissolution of the respect for this particular law was in rapid progress among the very class of citizens to whom an enlightened Government would look as the natural custodians of that respect for law as a whole which is an indispensable buttress of civilisation. The mind of the man or woman who becomes indifferent to any law of a country in which he or she lives may easily become warped in relation to other laws, civil, criminal, or moral. In the imperfection and frailty of human nature, one transgression easily and swiftly becomes the parent of another. But I am perhaps involving myself in a controversy not entirely necessary for the principal purpose of these notes.

Let me, then, summarise my conclusions. There has undoubtedly in the last twelve years been some relaxation in the standard of public morals. Such a decline is not rendered unimportant by the fact that it is principally to be discovered in the great cities of the world; for, after all, the aggregate population of these cities constitutes a vital element in the population of the world. But the deterioration must not be exaggerated. Its effect is not to be observed very much more in one country than in another; and there are already discernible some encouraging indications that its high-water mark has been reached.

IX

SIR EDWARD MARSHALL-HALL,
ONE OF HIS MAJESTY'S COUNSEL

THE subject of this notice was a very remarkable man. His death was not only an event in the legal world, but has attracted wide interest in the community generally. Indeed, if one were to take a list of the men who were called to the Bar by all the Inns of Court four years before and four years after Marshall-Hall, it is at least doubtful whether you could find one whose disappearance from the scene would have been more noticed or more regretted.

I first made his acquaintance twenty-three years ago, when he was the member for Southport, a young King's Counsel, and one of the most fashionable advocates of the day. He came down to Liverpool to lead me in a number of licensing briefs. The determined policy of the Liverpool justices at that time was to make a very great reduction in the number of licensed premises.

They were entirely right to do so. The greatest advocate who ever lived could not have deflected their intention. I knew this perfectly well, because I was familiar with the local conditions. And I so informed Marshall-Hall on the night of his arrival, in consultation at the old Adelphi Hotel. But an extraordinary sanguineness of disposition, which in many cases was a great support to him, made it impossible for him to accept, or to be guided by my view. He was receiving an enormous fee, which I happily shared, from the brewers, and felt certain that he could produce some impression upon the Bench.

When half his cases were finished—and he failed in every one—he rather dramatically announced that it was useless for an advocate to proceed, confronted by a travesty of justice; that he did not propose to continue taking part in a pre-arranged farce; and that he had advised his clients to carry the matter to Quarter Sessions.

I was not particularly pleased with this decision : first because it involved me in the labour, such as it was, of conducting the cases single-handed ; and secondly, because I knew perfectly well that we should get very little more satisfaction from Quarter Sessions that from the justices. And so in the event it proved.

I have always thought the incident illustrated very clearly the impetuosity of the man. Indeed, this quality was, perhaps, his greatest weakness. It led him into a series of conflicts with Judges, of which I will say more hereafter.

But the principal recollection I carried away of Marshall-Hall at this period of his life was his extraordinarily powerful and arresting physique. He was, indeed, one of the handsomest men whom I ever saw. Six feet three inches in height, powerfully and yet not clumsily built, skilful golfer and fine shot, he expressed in his distinguished features even a greater measure of force and intelligence than lay behind the appearance. To avoid the slightest appearance of disparagement in writing of an old friend, I make plain my view that no man could have been as wonderful as Marshall-Hall then looked.

At the time of which I speak, he seemed well within the running for Law Office. He was an attractive and powerful Parliamentary candidate, and had won Southport for the Conservative Party. He was continually in the forensic limelight, being constantly engaged in that class of case which interests the public, and, therefore, the Press. At that time many well-informed people in the lay and political world thought that Marshall-Hall might easily rise to the highest legal position of all.

And then, suddenly, a series of misfortunes befell him. He lost his seat at Southport in the difficult General Election of 1906. He lost it only to a very able and powerful opponent, the present Mr. Justice Astbury, and only by a narrow majority. The reverse, however, meant that he was denied any chance of sharing the exertions and the credit of the tiny band who held aloft the Conservative flag in the Mad Parliament of 1906.

But the disadvantage was apparent rather than real. Marshall-Hall did not, in fact, possess (he was the first to admit it) any of the necessary qualities for effective Parliamentary speech. In this respect he resembled an even greater advocate, the late Lord Russell of Killowen.

And coincidently with his political disappointment came a series of controversies with Judges before whom he had occasion to practise. It hardly ever pays a counsel to quarrel sharply with the Judge who is trying his client's case. It is no doubt sometimes necessary to do so,

especially in a matter tried by jury, where the
Judge has disclosed strong prejudice against the
advocate's side.   If the advocate is of very
great reputation ; the Judge of less, and clearly
wrong ; it may sometimes be the duty even of a
prudent advocate to carry the matter to the
stage of sharp controversy with the Judge.
But our Judges at *Nisi Prius* are to-day, and
have for so long been, of the highest personal
quality, that such occasions can seldom in practice arise.

That impetuosity of which I have spoken in
Marshall-Hall betrayed him at this particular
period into more than one Court scene, widely
reported, and very prejudicial to his reputation
and position at the Bar.   I remember, for instance, in the celebrated Goudie; case, he sat side
by side with the present Lord Reading.   Mr.
Justice Bigham, now Lord Mersey, was trying
the case.   He was not a Judge with whom anyone
could take liberties.   Marshall-Hall interrupted
the learned Judge, who replied sternly, " I have
already heard you, Mr. Marshall-Hall."   To which
the advocate, ill-advised, retorted, " Your Lord-
ship did not wish to hear me."

I shall not easily forget the severity with
which the Judge rebuked this observation ; and

I remember, too, that Rufus Isaacs whispered to Marshall earnestly, " Remember, we are sitting here, he is sitting there." In this incident Marshall was entirely wrong.

A little later he was confronted by a far more formidable conflict with a court of great authority, the Court of Appeal. The question arose whether Marshall-Hall had been justified in his method of conducting a case in the court below. The Court of Appeal took the view very strongly that his methods had been gravely irregular. I have myself always been of opinion that they exaggerated the whole matter, and that their censures were ludicrously overdone. I have reason also for believing that the most loyal of friends and admirable of advocates, whom we knew so long as Mr. Justice Montagu Lush, took the same view. He was a Bencher of Gray's Inn ; an advocate of commanding position at the Bar ; had been Marshall-Hall's junior in the court below ; and most warmly defended the reputation of his leader in the Court of Appeal. It was perhaps unfortunate that private differences notoriously existed between Marshall-Hall and that one of the members of the court who used the severest language. I have no doubt that the Court of Appeal on this occasion was guilty of a great injustice. If Marshall-Hall erred, it was from lack of technique. He was treated as a conscious delinquent. He never was one.

But the merits of the matter belong to the remote past. My immediate purpose is to describe the result. Widely reported, the criticisms withered, and for a prolonged period almost destroyed, Marshall-Hall's practice. I believe that it shrank from £15,000 or £16,000 a year to £1,000 or £2,000. Such a blow might have broken the proudest spirit, coming, as we have seen that it did, at the moment of his Parliamentary disappointment. And it was when suffering from this blow that Marshall-Hall showed himself a very great man ; and it is from this moment that a popularity with the Bar, which afterwards became extraordinary, commenced. He was always cheerful, always friendly ; he never complained to anyone of the bitter setback which he had experienced, or of the anxieties which at that time must have preyed upon his mind. He sold, it is true, one of the most curious and valuable collections of objects of art which any amateur at that time possessed and the possession of which was dear to his heart. But neither his mind nor his temper ever at any

moment seemed to become acid. I can see him
now, as I write, sitting at lunch in the Inner
Temple Hall, generally surrounded by the young
men in his Chambers, apparently in the highest
spirits of them all, gay and full of delightful
anecdote.

But it took years for him to regain the position
which he had lost. He did, however, fully regain
it. In the election—I think the second one—
of 1910 he was elected one of the members of
Parliament for Liverpool, and his practice at the
Bar, which had already showed signs of resiliency,
underwent rapid improvement : soon indeed his
own ascendancy in his own class of work became,
once again, undeniable.

The man whom I have described must evidently
have possessed remarkable qualities. For seventeen years after his return to Parliament he
maintained his position, often suffering from
ill-health, at the top of that very interesting
class of barristers who are engaged in the most
sensational and fashionable cases of the day.
In many of these cases he was remarkably successful ; and it may perhaps be moderately claimed
that there are men and women now at large who
owe much to his forensic gifts and were fortunate
in their exercise. He was certainly not among

the very greatest advocates. How few are! But a very high place must be given him in his day and generation. He was, in the first place, extraordinarily enthusiastic. Some of his cases were better than others, but he hardly ever had a really bad one. This habit of mind, if not indispensable, is certainly useful to a counsel who must continually argue difficult and doubtful cases. He derived from it a buoyancy and an apparent confidence in his client's case, which very often reacted upon and influenced the jury. And those advantages of personal appearance of which I have spoken were here of immense assistance. He often seemed to dominate the Court, throwing over his client the protection of his stately figure and striking features. He was not by any means a great speaker. His language was neither chosen with great taste nor expressed with great finish. But he was in the habit of addressing juries in a language which they understood, and with a vigour and cogency to which they very frequently reacted. He had a very concrete mind, and perhaps his strongest point was that he always most clearly grasped what the essential point in his own case was. And, having grasped it, he hammered away at it with iteration and reiteration, neglecting all else. The man who, arguing before juries, has learned this lesson, has mastered one of the elementary secrets of advocacy.

And his second great quality as an advocate was that he possessed great courage. This quality had something to do with his judicial quarrels. But surely it is an attractive quality (when so many play for safety) that a man should fling upon the table, in the interests only of his client, a counter which may be decisive in determining the whole future of his own professional life.

He never pretended to be a great or even a considerable lawyer. Unlike most good advocates who are bad lawyers, he was far too candid and too sure of himself to make any secret of this. And, in fact, I more than once heard him admit, sometimes half-jokingly, that his grasp of the technique of the law was pitiful. If a very technical matter arose in the course of a case, with which he felt himself ill-equipped to deal, he was far too great a man to make any secret of this fact. He would say openly and audibly to his junior: " This is more your line than mine ; will you take this point ? " The only other great advocate whom I have known in whom the same frankness was observable was the late Mr. Shee, K.C., of the Northern Circuit, who had many of Marshall-Hall's qualities, but with less earnestness and more humour.

The subject of this short sketch possessed in private life many most charming qualities. He was a loyal and devoted friend; and like so many members of the Bar, he was utterly incapable of professional jealousy. No one really ever went past him in his special line for all those long years in which he held the lists. But he often, of course, saw younger men climbing more rapidly that steep and difficult ladder which leads to the highest judicial advancement. In all the years that I knew him I never heard him speak in disparagement of these younger members of the profession who were storming the heights. And he often spoke of them with warm admiration.

It ought to be remembered, too, that his incredible flow of good spirits and his cheerfulness were maintained in the last ten years, while he struggled against a growing ill-health. He was always accustomed to physical exercise, and some affection of the veins in his legs made it necessary for him to give up every form of exercise to which he was accustomed: for the legs so affected were unable to support his great weight. I cannot doubt that his collapse was in some measure due to the enforced change in the habits of an active life.

He had at the end, in the mellow twilight of his career, become a universal favourite of Bench and Bar alike. And for many years, by special indulgence, he was permitted to conduct his cases sitting down, in order that his frame might be spared an unnecessary fatigue.

My own last interview with him took place only a few weeks before his death. He came to see me at my house to discuss a case in which a friend of mine was involved, and which it seemed to me ought in the interests of both parties to be adjusted without going to Court. I convinced him of the reasonableness of my view, and almost the last words I remember him saying were : "If my clients will not accept my advice, I shall tell them I can no longer act for them." I look back with great pleasure upon the long and intimate talk which, as old friends, we had on that day.

He had a long, stormy, and eventful life. He excited many animosities, but he lived to survive them. No one at the Bar had more friends, no one among the lay public more numerous or more ardent admirers. He died, I believe, without an enemy.

Warm-hearted ; much occupied ; at heart very simple ; a brave man ;

> "After life's fitful fever he sleeps well."

END OF VOLUME ONE